Rosita

Jayne

KU-276-028

Derith

Conolly

Avis

Rosalyn

Mariken

Elaine

Dee

the ♥ HAIRY BIKERS' BEST-LOVED RECIPES

Mums still know best!
xXx

the
HAIRY BIKERS'
BEST-LOVED
RECIPES

Mums still know best!
xXx

WEIDENFELD & NICOLSON

We'd like to dedicate this book to our dear friend Sammy-Jo

First published in hardback in Great Britain in 2011 by
Weidenfeld and Nicolson, an imprint of the Orion Publishing Group Ltd
Orion House, 5 Upper St Martin's Lane, London WC2H 9EA
an Hachette UK Company

10 9 8 7 6 5 4 3 2 1

Text copyright © Byte Brook Limited and Sharp Letter Limited 2011
Design and layout copyright © Weidenfeld & Nicolson 2011

A CIP catalogue record for this book is available from the British Library.

ISBN: 978 1 4072 3380 2

Photography by Cristian Barnett
Food styling by Sammy-Jo Squire
Design by Kate Barr
Edited by Jinny Johnson
Proofread by Elise See Tai
Index by Elizabeth Wiggans

Printed and bound in China

The Orion Publishing Group's policy is to use papers that are natural, renewable and recyclable and made from wood grown in sustainable forests. The logging and manufacturing processes are expected to conform to the environmental regulations of the country of origin.

www.orionbooks.co.uk

We enjoyed Mums Know Best so much we decided to do it all over again and discover some new recipes and yet more of Britain's great food!

As you probably know by now, we love good food and we love mums. So we've got on our bikes and toured round the country again, meeting more mums and their families and trying their great cooking. It's tough work but someone's got to do it! We've found loads more treasured recipes and we've sacrificed our waistlines to tuck into new puddings, pies and other delights. So many mums and their families have welcomed us into their homes to talk about the food they eat and what their recipes mean to them, and we've learned canny kitchen secrets from cooks the length and breadth of the British Isles.

For this new book, we've gathered lots of great recipes from the lovely mums, as well as some goodies from the community groups who came to party at the recipe fairs. We've also created more than 50 new recipes for our favourite dishes, some of which we've adored since childhood. We've taken a fresh look at these recipes – many of them cornerstones of British cooking – brought them up to date for today's cooks and made them as good as they can possibly be. They're recipes that will stand the test of time, recipes that reflect family traditions, and we want to share them with you.

There's a wealth of kitchen experience in this book, not only from us but also from the mums and their families. There are recipes for every day and for high days and holidays – everything from the milk pudding we remember from childhood to some of the best curries we've ever eaten. We hope you enjoy them all as much as we have – and don't forget, a little bit of what you fancy, when you fancy it, does you good!

love Si & Dave

Comforting
food

CREAM OF TOMATO SOUP
WITH FRIED CHEESE SANDWICHES

Memories from Dave's childhood – Saturday lunch with fried cheese sarnies and tinned tomato soup. This is still one of our favourite meals, but it's so much better with home-made soup.

SERVES 2

1 tbsp sunflower oil
1 large onion, roughly chopped
1 garlic clove, chopped
1 x 400g can of chopped tomatoes
½ tsp mixed dried herbs
2–3 tsp caster sugar
4 tbsp double cream
sea salt flakes
freshly ground black pepper

FRIED CHEESE SANDWICHES

4 slices of white bread
softened butter, for spreading
75g Cheddar cheese, coarsely grated
3 tbsp sunflower oil, for frying

To make the soup, heat the oil in a large saucepan and gently fry the onion and garlic for 5 minutes until they begin to soften. Stir in the tomatoes, then refill the can with water and pour it into the pan. Add the herbs, 2 teaspoons of the sugar, a good pinch of salt and plenty of freshly ground black pepper. Bring to a gentle simmer and cook for 15 minutes, stirring occasionally.

Remove from the heat and blitz the soup with a stick blender until it's as smooth as possible. Alternatively, let the soup cool for a few minutes, then blend it in a food processor and pour it back into the saucepan. Stir in the cream and adjust the seasoning to taste, adding a little more sugar if you think you need it.

To make the fried cheese sandwiches, spread the bread lightly with butter and put the cheese on 2 of the slices in an even layer, leaving a 1cm border around the edge. Top with the remaining slices of bread.

Heat the oil in a large non-stick frying pan over a medium-low heat. Carefully add the sandwiches to the pan and cook them for about 3 minutes on each side until golden brown and crisp. Warm the soup gently, stirring regularly.

When the sandwiches are done, remove them from the pan and cut into fingers or quarters. Ladle the soup into deep bowls and serve with the sandwiches.

For an extra touch of luxury, try making Italian fried cheese sandwiches with mozzarella.

ROUILLE & CROUTONS

Traditionally served as a spicy addition to fish soups and stews, this is a more sophisticated accompaniment to the cheese sarnies on the previous page. Rouille is like a butch mayonnaise and is great with the croutons – a grown-up version of the fried cheese sandwiches really! Please note: this recipe contains raw eggs.

SERVES 4

ROUILLE
3 dried chillies, deseeded
1 tsp coarse sea salt
4 garlic cloves, peeled
pinch of saffron
2 egg yolks
100–150ml olive oil
1 tsp lemon juice
pinch of cayenne pepper
chopped parsley or basil, for serving

CROUTONS
1 French stick
2 tbsp olive oil
knob of butter
150g Gruyère cheese, grated
cracked black pepper

First make the rouille. Grind the chillies into a powder in a pestle and mortar. Add the salt, garlic cloves and saffron and grind to a paste, then add the egg yolks. You should have a paste the colour of a jaundiced canary! Transfer this to a bowl.

Finishing the rouille is like making mayo. Very slowly, start to add the olive oil to the paste, a few drops at a time. When you've added half the oil, add the lemon juice and this will loosen the mixture. Continue drizzling in the oil and beat until you have a good consistency. Finish with the cayenne.

Next, make the croutons. Slice the bread. Heat the oil and butter together in a frying pan – the oil stops the butter burning and the butter ensures you end up with golden croutons. Fry the bread, a few slices at a time, until golden and set them on a baking tray.

When the croutons are all cooked, sprinkle them with grated Gruyère and season with black pepper. Put them under a hot grill until the cheese is melted and bubbling – you can melt the cheese with a cook's blowtorch if you prefer.

To serve, drop a crouton into the centre of each bowl of soup. Add a spoonful of rouille to the side and garnish with some chopped parsley or basil.

GREAT SAUSAGE CASSEROLE

A rich-tasting sausage casserole with a hint of spice, this is a great way to turn your favourite sausages into a main event. We like to add a dash of wine to the sauce, but it's very good without it too.

SERVES 6

1–2 tbsp sunflower oil
12 good meaty pork sausages
6 rindless streaky bacon rashers,
cut into 2.5cm lengths
2 medium onions, thinly sliced
2 garlic cloves, crushed
½–1 tsp hot chilli powder
or smoked paprika
1 x 400g can of chopped tomatoes
300ml chicken stock,
made with 1 chicken stock cube
2 tbsp tomato purée
1 tbsp Worcestershire sauce
1 tbsp dark brown muscovado sugar
1 tsp dried mixed herbs
2 bay leaves
3–4 sprigs of fresh thyme
100ml red or white wine (optional)
1 x 400g can of butter beans or
mixed beans
sea salt flakes
freshly ground black pepper

Heat a tablespoon of the oil in a large non-stick frying pan and fry the sausages gently for 10 minutes, turning every now and then until nicely browned all over. Transfer to a large saucepan or a flameproof casserole dish and set aside. Next, fry the bacon pieces in the frying pan until they begin to brown and crisp. Add to the sausages.

Put the onions in the frying pan and fry over a medium heat for 5 minutes until they start to soften, stirring often. You should have enough fat in the pan, but if not, add a little more oil. Add the garlic and cook for 2–3 minutes more until the onions turn pale golden brown, stirring frequently. Sprinkle over the chilli powder or smoked paprika and cook together for a few seconds longer.

Stir in the tomatoes, chicken stock, tomato purée, Worcestershire sauce, brown sugar and herbs. Pour over the wine, or some water if you're not using wine, and bring to a simmer. Tip carefully into the pan with the sausages and bacon. Return to a simmer, then reduce the heat, cover the pan loosely with a lid and leave to simmer very gently for 20 minutes, stirring every now and then.

Drain the beans and rinse them in a sieve under running water. Stir the beans into the casserole, and continue to cook for 10 minutes, stirring occasionally until the sauce is thick. Adjust the seasoning to taste. Serve with rice or slices of rustic bread.

Don't prick your sausages. The meat will cook better with the fat and the sausages will stay juicy.

MAMA'S CURRY

We met Anjie Mosher in Blackpool and she shared some of her mum's great recipes with us. This curry is one of her favourites and she told us that she used to invite her friends round for a curry – cooked by her mum Renee – on her birthday. Her friends always thought Anjie cooked the curry herself but now the secret's out! Sadly, Anjie's mum passed away four years ago, but Anjie says that when she cooks this recipe the smell makes her feel like she's just had a big hug from her mum.

SERVES 4

120ml ghee or vegetable oil
400g braising steak, diced
1 medium onion, diced
2 garlic cloves, finely chopped
1 tsp ground cumin
1 tsp ground coriander
1 tsp ground turmeric
1 tsp black pepper
1 tsp chilli powder
½ tsp ground ginger
3 cloves
3 cardamom pods (optional)
½ tsp ground cinnamon
200g canned tomatoes
125ml natural yoghurt
1 tbsp vinegar
1 tsp salt
pinch of sugar

Heat a frying pan and add the ghee or oil. Brown the meat until sealed on all sides, then take it out of the pan and set aside.

Add the onion and garlic to the pan and fry until soft but not browned. Add all the spices and fry for 1 minute, no longer.

Put the beef back in the pan with the tomatoes and bring to the boil. Take the pan off the heat and stir in the yoghurt and vinegar, then season with the salt and sugar. Place back on the heat, bring back to the boil and simmer for at least 1½ hours until the meat is tender.

Alternatively, if you prefer, you can cook the curry in the oven. Pile it into an ovenproof dish and cook in a preheated oven at 190°C/Gas 5 for at least 2 hours.

SPICED CAULIFLOWER

You have been warned – this recipe is very hot! If you want something milder Anjie says to halve the amount of spices used.

SERVES 4

60ml ghee or vegetable oil
2 tsp chilli powder
2 tsp ground cumin
2 tsp ground coriander
2 tsp turmeric
2 tsp black pepper
1 cauliflower, divided into florets
25g tamarind paste (optional)
1 tbsp vinegar
1 tsp salt

Heat a frying pan and add the oil. Add the spices and fry them over a medium heat for 2 minutes. Add the cauliflower and stir so all the florets are well coated with spice.

If you're using the tamarind paste, stir it into 250ml of boiling water and add this to the pan. If you don't have any tamarind just add 250ml of boiling water. Add the vinegar and salt and cook until the cauliflower is tender.

SWEET & SOUR POTATOES

Anjie told us how her mum always made these on her legendary curry nights and they are to die for. Great on their own or as a side dish with Mama's curry and the spiced cauliflower … yum!

SERVES 4

60ml oil
1 tsp black mustard seeds
1 tsp cumin seeds
6 medium potatoes, peeled and cubed
2 tsp ground coriander
2 tsp salt
1 tsp turmeric
1 tsp chilli powder
4 tsp brown sugar
250ml water
75g tomato purée
3 tbsp vinegar

Heat a frying pan and add the oil. Throw in the mustard and cumin seeds and fry them until they pop, then turn the heat down a little and add the potatoes. Add the remaining ingredients, pour in 250ml of water, then stir everything together well.

Cover the pan and cook over a low heat until the potatoes are tender. Take the lid off the pan and cook until the sauce has thickened.

REALLY RICH OXTAIL STEW

Your butcher will be able to get hold of a whole oxtail and cut it into portions for you. You should end up with at least 5 large pieces, a couple of slightly smaller joints and the little bits from the end of the tail. Cook the little pieces with the rest as they will add lots of flavour to the stew. Oxtails tend to be very fatty, so you'll need to trim your meat before you start cooking.

SERVES 5–6

1 whole oxtail (about 1.3kg),
cut into chunky pieces
3 tbsp plain flour
3–4 tbsp sunflower oil
2 medium onions, sliced
2 garlic cloves, finely chopped
2 medium carrots, peeled and diced
2 celery sticks, de-stringed and diced
4–5 bushy sprigs of fresh thyme
or ½ tsp dried thyme
2 bay leaves
300ml red wine
500ml beef stock
2 tbsp tomato purée
1 tbsp chopped fresh parsley leaves,
to garnish (optional)
sea salt flakes
freshly ground black pepper

Wash the oxtail pieces and pat them dry with kitchen paper. Trim off as much excess fat as possible. Put the flour in a freezer bag and season well with salt and pepper. Drop half the oxtail pieces into the seasoned flour, toss well to coat, then put them on a plate. Do the same with the remaining oxtail pieces.

Heat 2 tablespoons of the oil in a large non-stick frying pan. Brown the oxtail over a medium heat for about 10 minutes until deeply coloured, turning every now and then. You may need to add extra oil or cook the oxtail in batches depending on the size of your pan. Put the oxtail into a flameproof casserole dish.

Return the frying pan to the hob and add the onions, garlic, carrots and celery, with a little extra oil if necessary. Cook gently for 10 minutes until softened and lightly browned, stirring occasionally. Preheat the oven to 150°C/Gas 2.

Tip the vegetables on top of the beef and add the thyme and bay leaves. Stir in the wine, beef stock and tomato purée. Season with salt and pepper and bring to a gentle simmer. Cover the casserole dish with a lid and cook in the centre of the oven for 3 hours or longer, stirring and turning the oxtail halfway through the cooking time. The meat should be falling off the bones and the sauce should be rich and thick.

Remove the casserole dish from the oven and transfer the oxtail pieces to a plate. Using an oven glove, hold the dish up slightly at one side, allowing the sauce to run to the opposite side. Skim off the fat that has pooled on the surface and discard it.

Divide the oxtail pieces between six warmed plates and spoon over the sauce. Sprinkle with chopped parsley and serve with mash and fresh vegetables.

HOME-MADE FISH FINGERS

We know you've got a packet of fish fingers in the freezer, but try our home-made version. We guarantee they'll be the best you've ever tasted. And if you've had a hard day at work or school, put some between a couple of slices of bread, add some ketchup and all your troubles will melt away.

SERVES 4

500g thick skinless fillet of salmon or cod, haddock or other white fish
3 tbsp plain flour
1 large egg
50g golden breadcrumbs or 30g fresh white breadcrumbs, mixed with 20g easy-cook polenta
3 tbsp sunflower oil
sea salt flakes
freshly ground black pepper
bread, butter and ketchup, to serve

Cut the fish fillets into thick fingers – 4 really fat ones or 8 smaller ones, as you like. Don't worry if they're slightly strange shapes. They'll look all the better for it!

Put the flour in a strong freezer bag and season with a good pinch of salt and plenty of black pepper. Break the egg into a shallow dish and beat lightly. Put the breadcrumbs or breadcrumbs and polenta mix in a separate dish.

One at a time, gently toss the fish fingers in the seasoned flour until evenly coated. Next, turn them in the beaten egg until well covered, then dunk them in the breadcrumbs. Put them on a plate, ready to cook.

Pour the oil into a large non-stick frying pan and set over a medium-high heat. Add the fish fingers and fry for 5–6 minutes, turning occasionally until golden brown and crisp on all sides. Don't leave the pan of hot oil unattended.

Remove with a spatula and drain on kitchen paper. Serve in slices of freshly buttered bread with a good dollop of ketchup.

RUTH'S SHEPHERD'S PIE

Ruth Sutcliffe's family have lived in West Yorkshire for generations. They're upland sheep farmers and they need good comforting food to keep out the cold. Ruth still cooks from her Grandma Lassie's handwritten recipe book and she showed us some of her favourites. Grandma always added a handful of oats to thicken the meat stew and Ruth has continued that tradition – useful tip we thought.

SERVES 4–6

2 tbsp vegetable oil
1 large onion, chopped
2 carrots, finely chopped
2 celery sticks, finely chopped
450g minced steak
1 Oxo cube
2 tbsp porridge oats
150ml hot water
700g floury potatoes
butter and milk for the mash
salt and pepper

Heat the oil in a frying pan and fry the onion, carrot and celery until softened. Add the minced steak and fry until browned.

Crumble in the Oxo cube, season and continue to fry for about 10 minutes. Stir in the porridge oats and hot water.

Meanwhile, peel the potatoes, cut them into wedges and boil in salted water until tender. Mash with plenty of butter, milk and seasoning.

Preheat the oven to 180°C/Gas 4. Pile the meat mixture into an oven dish, top with the mash and cook in the oven until bubbling hot and brown on top – about 20 minutes.

GRANDMA SINDY'S GINGER SPONGE

Ruth's mum's mum – Grandma Sindy, also known as Nina – was an excellent baker and Ruth has many happy memories of Sunday tea at her house.

MAKES ABOUT 12 SQUARES

200g self-raising flour
200g sugar
1 tsp ground ginger
1 tsp bicarbonate of soda
55g margarine
1 egg, beaten
2 tbsp golden syrup
240ml hot water

Line a 28 x 18cm baking tin with baking parchment. Preheat the oven to 180°C/Gas 4.

Mix the flour, sugar, ground ginger and bicarbonate together in a bowl. Rub in the marge with your fingers, then add the beaten egg, syrup and hot water. Mix everything together well with a wooden spoon.

Pour the mixture into the prepared tin and bake in the oven for 35–40 minutes. Leave to cool in the tin and cut into squares when cold.

NINA'S ALMOND & COCONUT SLICE

Nina's tea table was always groaning with buns, cakes and sweet treats. It was all washed down with a proper cup of tea, made in a tea pot with tea leaves, of course.

SERVES AT LEAST 8

BASE
75g margarine
120g caster sugar
2 egg yolks
2 tbsp milk
1 tsp vanilla extract
170g self-raising flour

TOPPING
2 egg whites
120g caster sugar
55g desiccated coconut
10 glacé cherries, chopped
55g flaked almonds

Grease a 28 x 18cm baking tin and line it with baking parchment. Preheat the oven to 160°C/Gas 3.

Cream the margarine and sugar together until light and fluffy. Beat in the egg yolks, milk and vanilla, then fold in the flour. Spread the mixture into the lined tin – it will be very thick so you might need to use your hands.

To make the topping, whisk the egg whites until they form stiff peaks, then fold in the sugar and coconut. Spread this mixture over the base and sprinkle the cherries and almonds over the top. Bake in the preheated oven for 45 minutes, then leave to cool in the tin. Cut into slices when cold.

BAKED EGG CUSTARD & CUSTARD TART

**Eat this delicious baked custard as it is or put it into a
crisp pastry case to make a lip-smacklingly rich custard tart.**

SERVES 4

butter, for greasing
3 large eggs
2 large egg yolks
100g caster sugar
300ml double cream
300ml whole milk
½ tsp vanilla extract
½ whole nutmeg

PASTRY
200g plain flour
125g butter, cut into cubes
1 medium free-range egg, beaten

When mixing the eggs and egg yolks, use a wooden spoon rather than a whisk, as you don't want to incorporate bubbles into the mixture.

Preheat the oven to 150°C/Gas 2. Butter a 1.2 litre ovenproof
dish and set it in a small roasting tin. Bring a kettle of water to
the boil. Mix the eggs, egg yolks and sugar in a heatproof bowl
with a wooden spoon until smooth.

Put the cream and milk together with the vanilla extract in a
medium saucepan. Finely grate half the nutmeg over the mixture
and heat until hot but not boiling, stirring occasionally. Slowly
pour onto the eggs, stirring well. Pour the custard into the
prepared dish and grate the remaining nutmeg over the top.

Pour the just-boiled water into the roasting tin, until it rises no
more than a centimetre or so up the outside of the dish. Bake in
the oven for 25–30 minutes or until only just set. The custard
should be fairly wobbly in the centre, as it will continue to set
as it cools. Remove the tin from the oven, lift the dish from the
water and leave to cool. Chill for 2–3 hours before serving.

CUSTARD TART
To make the pastry, put the flour and the butter in a food processor
and pulse until the mixture resembles fine breadcrumbs. With
the motor running, gradually add the beaten egg and blend
until the mixture forms a ball.

Tip the pastry onto a floured board and roll to around 5mm
thick, turning the pastry and flouring the surface regularly.
Use to a line a 20cm loose-based cake tin. Trim the edges
neatly, prick the base lightly with a fork and chill the pastry
for 30 minutes. Preheat the oven to 200°C/Gas 6.

Put the tin on a baking sheet and cover the pastry with crumpled
baking parchment. Fill with baking beans. Bake the pastry blind
for 15 minutes, then remove the paper and beans. Return the
pastry to the oven for 3–4 minutes, then remove and reduce
the temperature to 160°C/Gas 3. Pour the custard into the pastry
shell, sprinkle with nutmeg and bake for 25–30 minutes until
set. Leave to cool, then slice and serve.

HARGREAVES'S MEAT & POTATO PIE

What could be more comforting than the biggest pie in the world? That's what Dee Briggs of Wakefield says, and she showed us how to make her dad's version of Denby Dale Pie, which he learned from his dad. Amazing! Her dad's recipe for special seasoning is lost, but Dee uses the mixture below. You need a big pie dish – 28 x 38cm – this is a crowd pleaser.

SERVES 12

2.75kg braising steak, diced
3 medium onions, chopped
30g salt
2.75kg potatoes, peeled and cut into chunks
5 tbsp special seasoning, made with
1 tbsp Bovril and 4 tbsp Bisto powder

PASTRY
1.5kg plain flour
30g salt
375g margarine
375g lard
beaten egg

Mix the diced beef and onions with the salt and place in a large pan. Pour in enough water to cover and bring to the boil. Put a lid on the pan and simmer for 2½–3 hours, or until the meat is really tender.

To make the pastry, put the flour and salt into a bowl. Dice the margarine and lard and add them to the flour. Process in a food processor or mix by hand until the mixture has the texture of breadcrumbs. Add 340ml of water and mix until the pastry forms a ball – add more water if needed. Leave the pastry in the fridge for 2 hours while the meat is cooking.

When the meat has been cooking for a couple of hours, cook the potatoes in salted water until tender. Drain and set aside, reserving the cooking water to make extra gravy.

Once the meat is cooked, remove the pan from the heat. Ladle some of the broth from the meat into a jug to cool. Once the broth has cooled, gradually add some of the gravy paste, mixing thoroughly all the time. Pour this gravy back into the meat and place the pan over a gentle heat. Once the meat is simmering, take the pan off the heat again.

Preheat the oven to 200C/Gas 6. Cut off a small amount of pastry and roll it out. Cut enough 4cm wide strips to edge the rim of the pie tin. Strain the meat and onions, reserving the gravy, then place in the tin in an even layer. Put the potatoes on top of the meat. Pour enough gravy over the filling in the pie tin to come to just under the potatoes – usually about 3 ladlefuls. Save the rest to make extra gravy to serve with the pie, thickening it with the rest of the gravy paste if necessary.

Roll out the rest of the pastry to the size of the tin. Brush the strips of pastry on the tin with beaten egg and place the pastry lid on top. Crimp the edges and brush the pie with beaten egg. Make a few slits in the top with a knife to allow the steam to escape. Cook in the preheated oven for 50–60 minutes.

Make the gravy paste, using 5 tablespoons of special seasoning mixed with 140ml of cold water (or potato cooking water). Stir until thoroughly mixed, then leave to infuse.

STEAMED SYRUP SPONGE PUDDING

This pud is comfort food heaven just as it is or you can vary the basic recipe by adding some cocoa, choc chips and orange zest to make a chocolate orange steamed pudding. Or try adding stem ginger and using honey instead of golden syrup.

SERVES 6

100g golden syrup, plus an extra
4–5 tbsp for serving
175g softened butter,
plus extra for greasing
125g golden caster sugar
grated zest of 1 lemon
3 medium eggs, lightly beaten
175g self-raising flour

Using golden syrup in the sponge batter as well as on top gives this pudding a more syrupy flavour and a light, open texture.

Generously butter the inside of a 1.2 litre pudding basin. Place the basin on a set of scales and spoon 50g of the golden syrup into the base. Set this aside. Put a large mixing bowl on the scales and add the remaining 50g of golden syrup, then the butter, sugar and lemon zest. Beat with an electric whisk until light and fluffy.

Whisk half the beaten eggs into the creamed mixture. Whisk in half the flour, then the remaining eggs and finally the rest of the flour. Spoon into the basin and smooth the surface.

Cover the dish with a large circle of baking parchment, with a pleat in the middle to allow for expansion. Cover the parchment with a circle of foil, again with a pleat. Tie both tightly in place with string. Create a carrying handle by tying the excess string across the top of the basin – this will help you lift the pudding out of the pan once it's cooked.

Place on an upturned heatproof saucer or small trivet in a large, deep saucepan and add enough just-boiled water to come halfway up the sides of the basin. (Alternatively, cook in a hob-top steamer.) Cover the pan with a tight-fitting lid and place over a low heat. Allow to steam in gently simmering water for about 1 hour and 45 minutes, adding more water if necessary.

When the pudding is done, turn off the heat and carefully lift the basin from the water. Leave to stand for 5 minutes. Cut the string from the basin and discard the foil and paper. Loosen the sides of the pudding with a round-ended knife and invert onto a deep plate.

Spoon over the extra syrup, which will warm up on contact with the sponge and run slowly down the sides of the pudding. Serve in generous wedges with custard (see page 211).

VEGGIE TABLE @ BATH PLACE COMMUNITY VENTURE

These recipes are from the Veggie Table Café, which is part of the Bath Place Community Venture in Leamington Spa. The Venture was established in 1974 and provides a wonderful centre for people in the area, with access to all kinds of facilities, support, information and education. There are workshops, classes and fun nights out, as well as places where you can meet and talk – something for everyone. These dishes are regulars on the café menu.

MUSHROOM SOUP

This tasty mushroom soup is easy to prepare and makes a lovely comforting lunch, served with some warm crusty bread.

SERVES 4

25g butter
1 large onion, finely chopped
1 green pepper, finely chopped
1 medium leek, finely chopped
1–2 garlic cloves, crushed
300g mushrooms, grated
2 tbsp plain flour
450ml vegetable stock
450ml milk
1 tbsp chopped parsley
sea salt flakes and black pepper

Melt the butter in a pan and fry the onion, pepper, leek and garlic until they start to soften. Add the mushrooms and continue frying until they are cooked.

Stir in the flour, then add the stock. Bring to the boil and allow the soup to simmer for a few minutes. Pour in the milk and bring back up to simmer. Season, stir in the chopped parsley and serve with crusty bread.

If you want a smoother consistency, blitz the soup in a blender after adding the milk.

MUSHROOM & SPINACH TAGLIATELLE

SERVES 4

1 tbsp olive oil
1 bunch of spring onions, finely chopped
2 garlic cloves, finely chopped
10 button or chestnut mushrooms, sliced
200g spinach, washed
1 tbsp plain flour
1 x 200ml tub of crème fraîche
300g tagliatelle
sea salt flakes and black pepper

Heat the oil in a pan and fry the spring onions and garlic for a few minutes. Add the mushrooms and fry for another 10 minutes. Add the spinach and allow to wilt, then continue cooking over a medium heat until most of the water has evaporated.

Sprinkle the flour over the mixture and stir it in well, then stir in the crème fraîche. Season, bring to the boil, then simmer for a few minutes.

Meanwhile, cook the pasta in plenty of boiling salted water according to the instructions on the packet. Drain, toss with the mushroom and spinach sauce and serve immediately.

Al fresco

LIL'S CHICKEN KIEV
WITH CUCUMBER & SPRING ONION SALAD

This is a recipe from Lil, Dave's missus, and it's one of her favourites. It's best if the chicken breasts aren't too large, so go for free-range ones, which tend to be smaller – and tastier.

SERVES 4

4 free-range chicken breasts, skin removed
150g butter, room temperature
1 bunch of fresh parsley, finely chopped
3 garlic cloves, crushed
2 spring onions, finely chopped
50g Cheddar cheese,
or any hard cheese in the fridge, grated
2 eggs, beaten
3 tbsp plain flour
3 tbsp golden breadcrumbs
sunflower oil, for deep-frying
sea salt flakes
freshly ground black pepper

CUCUMBER & SPRING ONION SALAD

2 cucumbers, peeled and cored
2 spring onions, chopped
50ml soured cream
1 tbsp mayonnaise
large pinch of paprika
2 hard-boiled eggs, sliced

Slit each chicken breast down one side and cut through almost to the other side so you can open the breast out like a book. Place it between 2 pieces of clingfilm and flatten with a rolling pin, then sprinkle with salt and pepper. Repeat with the other breasts and set them aside.

In a bowl, mix the butter, parsley, garlic, spring onions and grated cheese. Divide this stuffing into 4 and form each portion of stuffing into a baguette shape. Put the beaten eggs in a bowl and spread the flour and breadcrumbs on separate plates.

Next, prepare the salad. Using a vegetable peeler, cut the cucumbers into ribbons and mix with the spring onions, soured cream, mayonnaise and paprika. Garnish with the slices of hard-boiled egg.

Lay a chicken breast flat on a chopping board and place a portion of stuffing in the middle. Roll up the chicken very tightly around the stuffing and roll in the flour. Dip in the beaten egg, then roll in the breadcrumbs. Repeat with the remaining chicken breasts and stuffing.

Heat the oil in a deep-fat fryer to 160°C – you don't want the temperature too hot or the outside of the chicken will burn before the inside is cooked. Cook for about 15 minutes until the coating is golden and crispy and the chicken is cooked through. Serve with the salad.

TORTILLA

We met Rebecca Simpson-Hargreaves near Stockport where she lives, but she was born in Spain and still loves to cook the wonderful Spanish dishes she learned from her mum and her gran. This is her family's way of making tortillas.

SERVES 6
AS PART OF A TAPAS SELECTION

2 tbsp olive oil
1 large onion, sliced
vegetable oil for deep-frying
4 large potatoes, cut into thin slices
2 free-range eggs
½ tbsp salt

Heat the olive oil in a small frying pan and gently fry the onions until they are soft but not overly coloured. Transfer the onions to a bowl, then discard as much of the oil as possible.

Half fill a deep pan with vegetable oil and heat to 170°C or use a deep-fat fryer. When the oil is hot, add the sliced potatoes and cook until a fork goes through them easily – don't let them go crisp and brown. Put the cooked potatoes in the bowl with the onions and set aside. Beat the eggs for a few minutes until well mixed, then add the salt and beat again. Add the eggs to the potatoes and onions and gently mix with a fork to break up the potato slices.

Using the frying pan that you cooked the onions in, pour in the potato mixture and flatten it down. Leave to cook over a gentle heat for about 5 minutes. Once the tortilla is done, slide it onto a plate, cooked side down. Take your pan, place it over the non-cooked side, then gently turn everything over so the tortilla is back in the pan, cooked side up. Place the pan back on the heat and cook as before. When it's light brown underneath, take it off the heat. Tortilla is nice warm but best served cold.

TIO ROBERTO'S GAMBAS AL AJILLO

SERVES 6
AS PART OF A TAPAS SELECTION

4 tbsp extra virgin olive oil
3 garlic cloves, chopped
2 chillies (as hot or as mild as you like), deseeded and chopped
1 tbsp spicy paprika
½ onion, finely chopped
large bag of frozen prawns, defrosted, or a large handful of peeled fresh prawns

Heat the oil over a gentle heat and add the garlic, chillies, paprika and onion. Cook until the onions are soft, but don't let them brown.

Wash the prawns and add them to the oil for 5 minutes to cook through and add their flavour to the mixture. If you are using fresh prawns, cook them until each one turns dark pink – about 5–10 minutes. Rebecca likes to cook them for at least 10 minutes which gives the sauce a great flavour. Serve with crusty bread.

BOOMER'S ALBONDIGAS

Rebecca's brothers called their grandma Boomer – her real name was Mercedes.
She was a real character, apparently, and a great cook, but she didn't trust male chefs!

SERVES 6
AS PART OF A TAPAS SELECTION

500g minced beef or pork,
or a mixture of both
1 onion, finely chopped
4 garlic cloves, chopped
4 tbsp dried parsley (do not use fresh)
1 slice of bread, made into fresh breadcrumbs
1 free-range egg, beaten
plain flour
olive oil
2 carrots, quartered
and sliced into small triangles
1 tbsp paprika
generous pinch of saffron
½ tbsp salt

Put the minced meat in a bowl with half the chopped onion, 1 of the garlic cloves, 2 spoonfuls of parsley and breadcrumbs and mix with your hands. Squash everything together until well combined. Add the beaten egg and mix well to bind. Shape the mixture into small balls.

Sprinkle some plain flour round the edge of the mixing bowl and roll the meatballs in the flour until they are well coated. Heat a good glug of olive oil in a frying pan and add the meatballs, a batch at a time. Fry gently until crispy on the outside, then drain on kitchen towel. Continue until all the meatballs are cooked, topping up the oil as needed.

In the same pan, cook the carrots with the rest of the onions and garlic until the onions are soft and lightly coloured. Pour everything, including the oil, into a saucepan and place over a medium heat. Add the rest of the parsley, then the paprika, saffron and salt, and pour in a cup of water – about 300ml. Add the meatballs and warm through before serving.

PATATAS BRAVAS

SERVES 6
AS PART OF A TAPAS SELECTION

3 large potatoes, chopped into chunks
2 onions, chopped
olive oil
salt
1 tbsp sugar
1 garlic clove, chopped
6 ripe tomatoes, sliced
2 chillies, deseeded and chopped
spicy paprika

Parboil the potatoes until just cooked, drain and set aside to cool. Next make the sauce. Gently fry the onions in about a tablespoon of olive oil until soft, then season with salt and add the sugar. Add the garlic and tomatoes and simmer for about an hour. As the tomatoes are cooking, mash them from time to time with a potato masher or a spoon to break them down. When they're very soft, take them off the heat and press them through a sieve. Pour the sieved sauce back into the pan.

Add the chillies and a tablespoon of spicy paprika. If you like really spicy food, add more paprika and chillies to taste. Warm over a moderate heat for about 5 minutes. Fry the potatoes in olive oil until crispy, then drain on kitchen paper and put them into a bowl. Cover with the spicy bravas sauce and serve.

If you're short of time, you can cheat by buying some tomato frito sauce from the supermarket and adding paprika and chilli.

SPICED POTTED BEEF

A traditional potted beef recipe that's perfect for a picnic – delicious spread thickly onto fresh, crusty bread. There's a picture of the potted beef with the potted salmon over the page.

SERVES 4–6

100g butter
1 tsp freshly grated nutmeg
½ tsp ground ginger
½ tsp sea salt flakes
good pinch of cayenne pepper
2 garlic cloves, peeled
300g braising steak
freshly ground black pepper

PEPPERCORN TOPPING
25g butter
4 tsp green peppercorns in brine, drained

Preheat the oven to 150°C/Gas 2. Put the butter in a small saucepan and sprinkle over the nutmeg, ginger, salt, cayenne and garlic cloves. Season with lots of freshly ground black pepper and place over a low heat. Leave the butter to melt slowly, stirring occasionally.

Put the beef on a chopping board and trim off any hard fat or sinew. Cut the beef into 4 or 5 large chunks and place them in a small ovenproof dish. Pour the melted butter, spices and garlic over the top so that the beef is almost completely covered.

Place the dish on a baking tray and cover it with a tight-fitting piece of foil or a lid. Cook in the centre of the preheated oven for 3¼–3½ hours or until the beef is very soft. About halfway through the cooking time, remove the dish from the oven and turn the beef pieces over. Cover again and return to the oven for the remaining time.

At the end of the cooking time, take the beef out of the oven and remove the foil or lid. Press a chunk of the meat with a table knife – it should offer very little resistance. If the beef still feels a little firm, return to the oven for a further 20–30 minutes or so. Leave to cool for 30 minutes.

Tip the beef into a bowl with the garlic and buttery juices and mash until the mixture is as smooth as possible. Transfer to a small preserving jar or a ceramic bowl and spread evenly.

Melt the butter for the topping slowly in a small pan over a low heat. Spoon off any white foam that rises to the surface, then carefully pour the clarified butter onto the potted beef, leaving any sediment at the bottom of the pan. Scatter the peppercorns on top. Cover the jar or bowl and chill. Use the beef within 3 days.

POTTED SALMON

The inspiration for this and the potted beef on the previous page came from those dinky little jars of potted beef and salmon spread we remember from our youth. These are grown-up versions!

SERVES 6

2 x 150g skinless salmon fillets
1 small unwaxed lemon
1 bay leaf
50g butter
100g smoked salmon slices
100g full-fat soft cheese
small bunch of fresh dill, feathery leaves
stripped from the stalks
freshly ground black pepper
tiny bay leaves, snipped chives or dill sprigs,
to garnish

Put one of the salmon fillets in a small saucepan and pour over enough water to cover. Peel a wide strip of lemon zest using a vegetable peeler and add it to the pan. Drop the bay leaf into the pan and bring the water to a gentle simmer. Cover with a lid and cook for 6 minutes. Drain the salmon, transfer it to a plate and leave to cool.

Cut the second salmon fillet into small cubes, each roughly 1.5cm square – about the size of a dice. Put the cubes in a clean pan with the butter and set over a low heat. When the butter has melted, cook the salmon cubes for 2–3 minutes or until just cooked through, turning once. Remove from the heat and set aside.

Flake the poached salmon into chunky pieces and put in a food processor with the smoked salmon, soft cheese and dill sprigs. Finely grate the zest of half the lemon onto a board and scrape it into the food processor. Add plenty of black pepper.

Blend the fish mixture until almost smooth, removing the lid and pushing down once or twice with a rubber spatula. Transfer the mixture to a bowl. Using a slotted spoon, add the cooked salmon cubes, reserving the melted butter, and fold them in very gently.

Spoon the salmon mixture into a preserving jar or small ceramic dish. Pour over the melted butter (used to cook the salmon cubes), leaving any sediment at the bottom of the pan. Garnish with tiny bay leaves, snipped chives or sprigs of dill, cover and leave to set in the fridge. Eat within 2 days.

Make our quick melba toast to go with this. Just toast some white sliced bread and split the slices in two.

STUFFED CABBAGE

Marika Gallimore and her brother Karl are from Hungary, although they were born in Britain, and they like to keep their Hungarian heritage alive through food. They took us on a camping trip and showed us how to cook some traditional Hungarian dishes over the camp fire. Wonderful stuff!

SERVES 10

1 large white cabbage
40g lard
1 large onion, chopped
2 tbsp paprika
1.4kg minced pork
450g long-grain rice
1 x 400g can of tomatoes
soured cream, to serve
salt and pepper

Put the cabbage in a large pan, add hot water and boil until the leaves fall off the cabbage. Put the leaves on a plate to drain and cool.

Melt the lard in a frying pan, then add the chopped onion and fry until soft. Take the pan off the heat, tip the onions into a bowl and stir in the paprika, adding more or less as required. Add the minced pork and the rice, then season to taste and mix well.

Take a cabbage leaf and cut away a little of the stalk so that it is easy to roll. Add a spoonful of the mincemeat mixture to the stalk end of the leaf, then roll the cabbage into a sausage shape, tucking in the ends. Try to roll the leaf as firmly as possible, so that it doesn't unroll during cooking. Continue until you have used all the stuffing mixture.

Shred any leftover cabbage and use it to line the bottom of a large pan – this prevents the stuffed cabbage leaves from burning. Place the stuffed leaves in the pan as snugly as possible, then cover with some more shredded cabbage.

Add boiling water to cover, bring to the boil, and then add the tomatoes and more seasoning. Allow the cabbage to simmer for 1–1½ hours, until the pork is cooked.

Serve the stuffed cabbage drizzled with the juices of the cabbage and topped with soured cream. Good with some crusty bread too.

PÖRKHÖLT

Pörkölt is an Hungarian meat stew, also known as Perka. Shepherds used to make this in a cauldron over an open fire when they were out on the plains and many Hungarians still like to cook it this way. The stew can be made with beef, veal or chicken as well as pork.

SERVES 8–10

40g lard
1 large onion, thinly sliced
2–3 tbsp paprika
1.8kg pork steak, diced
1 tsp tomato purée
1 green pepper, thinly sliced
3 medium tomatoes, sliced
1 tbsp cornflour
salt and pepper

Heat the lard in a frying pan and fry the onion until soft. Take the pan off the heat and stir in the paprika, adding more or less to suit your taste.

Add the pork steak and a little boiled water to keep the meat moist as the juices release. Simmer over a low heat for about 5 minutes to seal in the flavour. Add enough boiled water to cover the meat, bring back to the boil and add the tomato purée, green pepper, sliced tomatoes and seasoning. Cover with a lid to keep the moisture in and simmer for about 1 hour until the pork is tender.

To thicken the sauce, add the cornflour to cold water and mix to form a paste, then stir this into the stew. Bring to the boil again to thicken. Serve with creamy mashed potatoes or macaroni and a side dish of finely sliced cucumber in white wine vinegar and sugar.

SALMON & DILL FISHCAKES
WITH HOLLANDAISE SAUCE

These fish cakes are the best, full of juicy flakes of salmon. The mash needs to be really dry, so place the pan over a low heat while you mash the potatoes but make sure they don't burn.

MAKES 8

800g skinless salmon fillets
2 bay leaves
small bunch of dill, stalks and fronds separated
500ml whole milk
600g Maris Piper potatoes, peeled and chopped into even-sized pieces
grated zest of 1 lemon
4 tbsp mayonnaise
1 tsp Dijon mustard
1 tsp paprika
4 tbsp salted capers, rinsed and dried
plain flour, for dusting your hands
handful of parsley, chopped
100g breadcrumbs
1 egg
vegetable oil, for shallow frying
white pepper
sea salt to taste

HOLLANDAISE SAUCE
225g butter
4 tbsp white wine vinegar
1 small shallot or ½ banana shallot, finely chopped
10 black peppercorns
1 bay leaf
3 large egg yolks
pinch of sea salt
pinch of caster sugar

Put the salmon fillets in a frying pan with the bay leaves and dill stalks. Pour over enough milk to cover the fish. Bring the milk to the boil, then lower the heat to a gentle simmer and leave the fish to poach for 4 minutes. Turn off the heat and leave the fish to continue cooking in the poaching liquid for a couple of minutes longer. Lift the salmon out onto a plate. Flake into large pieces with a fork, then leave to cool.

Boil the potatoes in salted water until tender. Drain well, then leave to cool for a couple of minutes before putting them back into the pan and mashing them. Stir in the zest, dill fronds, mayonnaise, mustard, paprika and capers. Season to taste.

Pat away any liquid from the fish with kitchen paper, then gently fold the fish into the mash with your hands until roughly combined. Try not to break up the flakes. Dust your hands with flour and shape a handful of the mix into a cake, about 2.5cm thick. Repeat until you've used up all the mix.

Mix the parsley and breadcrumbs in a bowl and beat the egg in a separate bowl. Dip the cakes into the egg, then press into the breadcrumbs and parsley mix, making sure they are well covered. Heat the oil in a frying pan and fry a few of the fishcakes for 5 minutes on each side until golden. Remove and keep them warm while you fry the rest.

HOLLANDAISE SAUCE
Melt the butter slowly in a pan over a low heat, stirring occasionally. Remove from the heat and pour into a jug. Put the vinegar, shallot, peppercorns and bay leaf in a small pan over a high heat and bring to the boil. Cook for 1–2 minutes until the liquid has reduced to about 2 tablespoons.

Put the egg yolks in a heatproof bowl and place over a pan of simmering water. Whisk the egg yolks with the salt and sugar until pale. Pour the vinegar reduction through a fine sieve onto the yolks and continue whisking until thoroughly combined. Gradually, add the hot butter in a steady stream, whisking constantly until the sauce is thick and shiny.

MINCED BEEF PINWHEELS

**Another triumph with ready-made puff pastry – these help a small amount of meat go a long way.
Fun to make with the kids.**

MAKES 12

1 tbsp sunflower oil
½ medium onion, peeled and
very finely chopped
1 garlic clove, peeled and crushed
500g lean minced beef
1 tsp dried mixed herbs
(preferably freeze-dried)
1 tbsp tomato purée
1 tbsp plain flour, plus extra for rolling
500g block of ready-made puff pastry
50g mature Cheddar cheese, finely
grated (optional)
1 medium egg, beaten
sea salt flakes
freshly ground black pepper

Preheat the oven to 200°C/Gas 6. Line a large baking tray or
2 smaller baking trays with baking parchment. Heat the oil
in a small frying pan and gently fry the onion and garlic for
2–3 minutes until soft, stirring regularly. Tip the mixture into
a large heatproof bowl and leave to cool for few minutes.

Add the minced beef, dried herbs, tomato purée and a tablespoon
of flour to the bowl with the onion and season well with salt
and pepper. Mix with your clean hands until thoroughly
combined.

Roll out the pastry on a lightly floured surface into a roughly
34 x 34cm square. Spread the mince mixture over the pastry,
leaving a 2cm border around the edges. Sprinkle on the grated
cheese, if using, and brush the pastry edges with a little of the
beaten egg. Roll up smoothly and firmly, like a Swiss roll.

Cut the roll into 12 slices using a serrated knife – a bread
knife is ideal. Place the pinwheels on the baking tray (or
trays), spaced well apart to allow for rising. Flatten slightly
with the palm of your hand. Brush the pastry sides with
more beaten egg to glaze. Bake for 15 minutes or until well
risen and golden brown. Best served warm.

You can also make a chicken, sage and onion filling or even use left-over bolognese sauce.

MUM'S PLUM SUMMER PUDDING

We met Jayne Rawlings in Lincoln. She gave us this recipe, which is a Victorian dinner party classic and has been handed down through four generations of her family. Jayne enjoys walking and likes to use wild fruits, and other goodies she finds and picks, in her cooking.

SERVES 8

750g dark red or black plums
120g caster sugar
2 tbsp sloe gin, damson vodka or cassis (optional)
½ – ¾ medium white sliced loaf, crusts removed

Remove the stones from the plums and cut them into quarters. Place the plums in a large pan with about 5 tablespoons of water and add the sugar. Heat to dissolve the sugar, shaking the pan frequently so that the fruit doesn't stick to the bottom and burn. Continue to cook the plums, uncovered, until they are soft and have released lots of juice. Taste and add more sugar if necessary and the liquor if using.

Cut the corners off one slice of bread to make a rough circle. Dip it in the plum juice and place it, wet side down, at the bottom of a pudding basin. Cut some more slices of bread in half, dip each one in the juice and place them up the sides of the basin – wet sides outwards. Now cut a second circle of bread and place it on top of the other base piece to keep the sides in place.

Pour the fruit and juice into the bread-lined basin, filling it right to the top. Take 4 more slices of bread and cut an arc on one side of each to fit the curve of the basin rim. Place these shaped slices on top of the fruit. Cover tightly with clingfilm and invert onto a plate, then place in the fridge for at least a day.

When ready to serve, turn the basin right side up again and remove the clingfilm. Run a knife around the edge of the pudding and then invert the basin to turn the pudding out onto a deep wide dish. The pudding will sag with the weight of fruit, but don't worry. Cut into wedges and serve with crème fraîche.

If you make this pudding with little wild plums, you'll find it easiest to cook them whole, then pick out the stones. You can also use other seasonal fruits, such as apples, strawberries, gooseberries and blackcurrants.

MUD PIE

This is an amazing pudding recipe that Jayne's mum used to cook for her family and Jayne still makes today. The family called it mud pie because … well, it looked like mud! It's an original and Jayne says she has never seen anything like it in any cookbook.

SERVES 6

200g dark chocolate, at least 70 per cent cocoa solids
100ml strong coffee, cooled, or Camp coffee essence
600ml double cream
4 tbsp milk
200g marshmallows

BISCUIT BASE
200g digestive biscuits
75g butter

First make the biscuit base. Put the biscuits in a freezer bag and crush them with a rolling pin. Gently melt the butter in a pan, add the crushed biscuits and mix together. Tip the mixture into a 25cm flan dish and press down well. Set aside to cool.

Break the chocolate up into chunks and place them in a bowl set over a pan of simmering water. Make sure the bowl doesn't touch the water. Allow the chocolate to melt, then stir in the coffee or coffee essence. In a separate bowl, whip the cream to soft peaks, taking care not to whip it too much.

Put the milk in a pan and add the marshmallows. Stir continuously over a very low heat until the marshmallows have melted into the milk, making a wonderfully gooey mixture. Remove from the heat and stir in the melted chocolate, a tablespoon at a time, mixing well. Beat in the cream, using a balloon whisk to remove any lumps. Pour the mixture onto the biscuit base and leave it in the fridge for about 8 hours to set. To jazz this recipe up for special occasions, you can add 3 tablespooons of dark rum with the coffee essence.

HOME-MADE LEMONADE

MAKES A LARGE JUGFUL

10 organic lemons, well scrubbed
100g citric acid
2.25kg caster sugar

Slice the lemons thinly, removing any pips. Place the slices in a large heatproof jug and add the citric acid. Tip in the caster sugar, then pour in 1.2 litres of boiling water. Leave to cool, then sieve. Chill and dilute with water or soda to triple quantities or to taste. Serve with ice and some fresh lemon slices if you like.

CINDER TOFFEE

A bonfire night treat for all the family. Watch the cooking times and temperature closely to be sure you end up with light, bubbly cinder toffee (honeycomb) that holds its shape as it cools. A sugar thermometer is a big help and remember to take great care – molten toffee can cause nasty burns.

MAKES ABOUT 20 CHUNKY PIECES

softened butter, for greasing the tin
2 tsp bicarbonate of soda
350g caster sugar
200g golden syrup
75g butter
2 tbsp white wine vinegar
200g dark or milk chocolate,
broken into squares

Butter a 25cm square loose-based brownie tin, or cake tin, and line it with baking parchment. Make sure you take the parchment paper right up the sides, so the edges of the toffee can't stick. Set aside. Measure the bicarbonate of soda into a small bowl and have a large metal, balloon whisk standing by.

Put the sugar, golden syrup, butter and vinegar into a large saucepan. Add 200ml of cold water and set the pan over a low heat. (You'll need a large pan because the cinder toffee will bubble up and could overflow.) Stir occasionally until the sugar has completely dissolved.

Place a clip-on sugar thermometer into the pan. The sugar syrup will be heated to an extremely high temperature, so don't be tempted to touch or taste at any stage. Increase the heat under the pan to medium-high and bring the sugar syrup to the boil. Stir once with a wooden spoon, then leave the toffee boiling until it reaches 154°C or the hard crack stage on your thermometer. We found that 158°C gave the best results, so watch carefully.

Taking great care, remove the pan from the heat and place it on a heatproof surface. Sprinkle over the bicarbonate of soda and immediately whisk very lightly with a large metal whisk to combine the soda with the toffee. The toffee will bubble ferociously and rise in the pan. Leave for a few seconds, then while it is still bubbling, pour the mixture gently into the prepared tin, allowing it to flow to all the sides. Leave to cool for 15 minutes. Using a lightly oiled knife, deeply score the cinder toffee into 20 squares. Leave to cool completely.

Melt the chocolate in a heatproof bowl over a pan of gently simmering water, or in the microwave, until smooth. Carefully remove the cinder toffee from the tin and put it on a board. Peel off the baking parchment. Cut the toffee into chunky squares. Place on a wire rack above a plate and spoon over the melted chocolate, allowing it to dribble down the sides.

If you don't have a sugar thermometer, have a large mug of very cold water beside the hob. Drip a little hot toffee from a long-handled spoon into the water. If it's ready, it will form thin brittle threads that harden immediately.

If you use milk chocolate, you'll find it easier to dip the pieces of toffee into the chocolate, as milk chocolate doesn't run as freely as the dark chocolate.

STUDLEY GROW, COOK & EAT

This lottery-funded arts and health project is based on growing, cooking and eating fresh seasonal fruit and vegetables and was developed by Escape: Community Art in Action, a Warwickshire arts charity. The project enables people to 'feed' their passion for local food and has developed a fantastic community programme of cooking and creative environmental arts.

RICOTTA HOT CAKES
WITH PLUM COMPOTE

Abi Macfarlane, from Studley Grow, Cook and Eat, gave us this recipe. The hot cakes are as light as air and make a delicious brunch, especially when served with a fruity plum compote.

SERVES 10

4 eggs, separated
180ml milk
½ tsp vanilla essence
225g ricotta
2 tbsp caster sugar
140g plain flour
1 tsp baking powder
½ tbsp sunflower oil

PLUM COMPOTE
700g plums, halved and stoned
50g caster sugar
1 cinnamon stick

First make the compote. Cut each plum half into 3 or 4 pieces and put them in a small pan with the sugar and cinnamon stick and a little water. Cook over a moderate heat, stirring occasionally until the plums are soft.

In a bowl, whisk together the egg yolks, milk, vanilla, ricotta and sugar. Mix the flour and baking powder together, then add this to the ricotta mixture. Whisk the egg whites to soft peaks and fold them into the mixture.

Heat the oil in a frying pan. Using a serving spoon, add a few dollops of the ricotta mixture into the pan. When the surface starts to bubble, turn the ricotta cakes and cook on the other side. You should get about 30 hot cakes from this mixture. Serve with plum compote and crème fraîche.

PORT & PLUM SAUCE

This is a lovely versatile sauce recipe from Karen Jones. It can be used to make the plum chocolates opposite or to accompany any sweet dish – truly scrumptious.

MAKES A GOOD BOWLFUL

30g unsalted butter
450g chopped plums
5½ tbsp light brown sugar
125ml ruby port
pinch of freshly grated nutmeg (optional)

Melt the butter over a medium heat. Add the plums and sauté for 2–3 minutes until they begin to soften. Add the sugar and cook for 4–5 minutes until the sugar begins to caramelise. Stir in the port and simmer over a low heat for 3–5 minutes until slightly thickened. Remove from the heat and stir in the nutmeg, if using. The sauce can be prepared and refrigerated for up to 24 hours in advance. Serve at room temperature.

KAREN'S PLUM CHOCOLATES

MAKES 24

DARK PLUM CHOCOLATES
170g dark chocolate
4 tbsp port and plum sauce (see opposite)

RICH PLUM BITES
30g butter
handful of peeled and chopped plums
2 tbsp light brown sugar
170g dark chocolate
4 tbsp port and plum sauce (see opposite)
handful of chopped Brazil nuts (optional)

Melt the chocolate in a bowl over a pan of simmering water. Add the plum and port sauce and mix well. Spoon into small paper chocolate cases and refrigerate until firm.

RICH PLUM BITES
Melt the butter over a medium heat, add the plums and sauté until they begin to soften. Add the sugar and cook until it begins to caramelise, forming a syrup. Remove from the heat.

Prepare the chocolate and port and plum sauce mix as above, then add the caramelised plums. Top with some chopped Brazil nuts, too, if desired. Spoon into small paper chocolate cases and chill before eating.

Taste
of home

SPAGHETTI BOLOGNESE

The long, slow cooking of this sauce tenderises the meat and allows the flavours to bubble through. We know it's not traditional, but we find that adding a touch of flour at the beginning prevents the bolognese sauce looking watery when it's served.

SERVES 5–6

500g lean minced beef
1 medium onion, finely chopped
2 celery sticks, trimmed and finely sliced
2 medium carrots, finely diced
2 garlic cloves, finely chopped
150g small portobello or chestnut mushrooms, wiped and sliced
1 tbsp plain flour
150ml red wine
1 x 400g can of chopped tomatoes
2 tbsp tomato purée
1 beef stock cube
1 tsp caster sugar
1 tsp dried oregano or
1 tsp dried mixed herbs
2 bay leaves
375–450g dried spaghetti
freshly grated Parmesan cheese, for serving
sea salt flakes
freshly ground black pepper

Put the mince in a large non-stick saucepan with the onion, celery, carrots and garlic. Dry fry over a medium heat for 8–10 minutes or until the beef is no longer pink and the vegetables are beginning to brown. Stir the meat with a wooden spoon to break up any large clumps. Add the mushrooms and fry with the mince and vegetables for another 2–3 minutes. Sprinkle over the flour and stir well.

Stir in the wine and add the tomatoes and tomato purée, along with 300ml of cold water. Crumble the stock cube over the top, then add the caster sugar and herbs. Season with a few twists of black pepper, give a good stir and bring to a simmer. When the liquid is bubbling, reduce the heat and simmer very gently for 30–40 minutes, without covering, stirring occasionally.

Half fill a large pan with water and bring to the boil. As soon as the water is boiling, add the spaghetti and push it down with a wooden spoon to encourage the strands to separate. It's important to use lots of water, so the spaghetti can move freely without sticking together. Cook for 10–12 minutes, or according to the packet instructions.

While the spaghetti is cooking, increase the heat under the sauce and simmer for another 10 minutes or until the liquid is well reduced and the sauce looks rich and thick. Stir regularly and adjust the seasoning if necessary.

Drain the spaghetti in a colander and divide between warmed bowls. Spoon the bolognese mixture on top, sprinkle with freshly grated Parmesan cheese and serve immediately. If serving at the table, it's a good idea to toss the spaghetti with a tiny amount of oil before transferring it to a serving dish. This will stop the pasta sticking. Make sure you don't add too much though, or the sauce will slide off the spaghetti.

Mix half a haggis in with the beef to create a spicier sauce that we call hag bog!

MACARONI CHEESE

This is a classic – every home should have one. Don't be pedantic about the cheese and take the opportunity to use up all those little hard scraps in the fridge. They'll taste just as good.

SERVES 4

250g macaroni
50g butter, plus extra for greasing
50g plain flour
500ml whole or semi-skimmed milk
150g mature Cheddar cheese, finely grated
4 medium tomatoes, sliced
sea salt flakes
freshly ground black pepper

Preheat the oven to 200°C/Gas 6. Half fill a large saucepan with water and bring it to the boil. Add the macaroni and return to the boil. Cook for 8–10 minutes, or according to the packet instructions, stirring occasionally.

While the pasta is cooking, prepare the sauce. Melt the butter in a medium non-stick saucepan over a low heat, then stir in the flour and cook for 30 seconds, stirring constantly.

Gradually stir in the milk and bring to a gentle simmer. Cook for 3 minutes until the sauce is thickened and smooth, stirring constantly. Add roughly two-thirds of the cheese and season with salt and ground black pepper. Cook for 2–3 minutes more and keep stirring. Add a little more seasoning if necessary.

Drain the pasta in a large colander and return it to the pan. Gently stir in the hot cheese sauce until thoroughly combined. Tip the macaroni cheese mixture into a large, buttered ovenproof dish – a lasagne dish is ideal – and spread it to all the corners.

Sprinkle with half the remaining cheese and arrange the sliced tomatoes on top, discarding the ends. Sprinkle with the rest of the cheese and add a couple of twists of ground black pepper. Bake for 20–25 minutes until the tomatoes are softened and the cheese is lightly browned. Serve with some lovely fresh bread and butter.

If you like, fry some button mushrooms in a little butter until golden. Stir them into the cooked pasta before adding the sauce. Si likes to add bits of fried bacon too, so give that a try.

SALTFISH & ACKEE
WITH FRIED DUMPLINGS

Julia Titus lives in Reading and her dad is from Jamaica. He came to England in the 1950s but didn't take to English food so taught his family how to cook Jamaican-style. Julia showed us some great Jamaican classics.

SERVES 4

450g salt cod
1 x 400g can of ackee
olive oil
1 onion, chopped
1 tsp paprika
2 tsp mild curry powder
2 tsp jerk seasoning
1 tsp hot pepper sauce
1 red and 1 yellow pepper, sliced
200g tomatoes, chopped
salt and black pepper

DUMPLINGS
250g self-raising flour
30g vegetable suet
pinch of salt
vegetable oil, for frying

Soak the salt cod overnight, changing the water a couple of times. Drain, then put it in a large pan of fresh water and bring to the boil. Drain, add fresh water and bring to the boil again. Simmer for about 5 minutes until cooked through, then drain and flake the fish into large pieces. Discard any skin or bones.

For the dumplings, mix the flour and suet with a pinch of salt and 250ml water to make a dough. Wrap the mixture in clingfilm and leave in the fridge to rest. Open the can of ackee, drain and rinse, then leave to one side.

Heat a tablespoon of olive oil in a pan and fry the onion until softened. Add the spices, seasoning and pepper sauce, then the sliced peppers and continue to fry until the peppers are tender. Add the chopped tomatoes, then the salt cod and mix together. Lastly stir in the ackee very gently and leave to simmer until ready to serve.

When you're almost ready to eat, heat some vegetable oil in a frying pan and shallow fry the dumplings until golden. Serve with the salt cod stew.

SMASHED-UP CHICKEN
WITH GARLIC & CHILLI PASTA

This is a lovely lemony chicken dish, served with chilli-spiked pasta – perfect Mediterranean-fresh flavours and a real taste of summer. Use whatever pasta shapes you fancy, but we find that fusilli works well. Bashing the chicken is a fantastic way to let out all your pent-up emotions.

SERVES 4–6

2 large chicken breasts, skinned
3 tbsp plain flour
2 tbsp olive oil
150g fresh wild mushrooms, chopped
150ml dry white wine
75ml chicken stock
2 garlic cloves, crushed
1 tbsp chopped fresh tarragon
1 tbsp lemon juice
finely grated zest of 1 lemon
2 tbsp capers (rinsed)
2 tbsp crème fraîche
handful of flat-leaf parsley, chopped
fine sea salt
freshly ground black pepper

GARLIC & CHILLI PASTA
250g pasta, such as fusilli
2 tbsp olive oil
1 tbsp chilli flakes
2 garlic cloves, crushed
Parmesan cheese, to finish

First the fun bit: put a chicken breast between two pieces of clingfilm and beat it with a rolling pin until super thin. We want the chicken all smashed up for this – we don't want schnitzels or escalopes. Remove the top piece of clingfilm and peel off the ribbon-like fragments of chicken. Repeat with the other chicken breast. Season the flour with salt and pepper and roll the chicken bits in the flour.

Heat the oil in the frying pan and cook the chicken until golden and just cooked through. Remove the chicken from the pan and set aside. Fry the mushrooms in the remaining oil, adding a drop more if it looks a bit dry. Set them aside with the cooked chicken.

Pour the wine and stock into the pan and bring to the boil to deglaze all the sticky bits from the bottom of the pan. Cook for a couple of minutes to reduce the liquid, then add the garlic, tarragon, lemon juice and the zest. Cook for 2 minutes, then add the capers.

Remove from the heat and whisk in the crème fraîche, then return the chicken and mushrooms to the pan to warm through. Finish off with the chopped parsley and check the seasoning.

Cook the pasta in plenty of salted boiling water according to the instructions on the packet. Meanwhile, heat a tablespoon of the oil in a frying pan and fry the chilli flakes and garlic. Drain the pasta well, then add the chilli-garlic oil and another tablespoon of oil. Check the seasoning, add the Parmesan cheese and serve with the chicken

Great with a glass of chilled dry white wine and a green salad.

WELSH CAKES

Mary Hamilton lives in Surrey now, but she told us that her heart is still in Wales, where she grew up. Mary learned to cook from her nan and this is one of her favourites – something she and her sons like to enjoy when they're watching Welsh rugby on TV. Apparently, lots of people come round to join them and Mary's not sure if it's the rugby they like or the teatime treats. We think we know!

MAKES 6–8

225g self-raising flour
110g salted butter, diced
85g caster sugar, plus extra for dusting
handful of sultanas
1 egg, beaten
milk, if needed
extra butter, for greasing

Sift the flour into a bowl and add the diced butter. Rub with your fingertips until the mixture has the texture of breadcrumbs. You can do this in a food processor if you prefer.

Add the sugar, dried fruit and beaten egg. Mix well to form a ball of dough, using a splash of milk if needed. Roll the dough out to a thickness of about 5mm. Cut into rounds with a 7.5–10cm plain cutter.

Cook the cakes on a heavy iron griddle or a bakestone. Rub the griddle with butter and wipe away any excess. Heat, then add the Welsh cakes a few at a time and cook for 2–3 minutes on each side, until golden brown. Remove from the griddle and dust with caster sugar while still warm.

LIVER & BACON
WITH ONIONS & GRAVY

A great dish that mums used to cook every week when we were young. This is best made with lambs' liver, but if you're feeling posh, use calves' liver instead and simmer the onions with a good slurp of marsala wine instead of making a traditional gravy.

SERVES 4

450g lambs' liver, sliced and
fully thawed if frozen
25g butter
1 tbsp sunflower oil
2 tbsp plain flour
1 onion, peeled,
halved lengthways and sliced
125g rindless streaky bacon rashers,
each cut into 4–5 pieces
1 beef stock cube
500ml just-boiled water
1–2 tsp tomato ketchup
sea salt flakes
freshly ground black pepper

Rinse the liver in a colander under cold water and drain well on kitchen paper. Melt half the butter with the oil in a large non-stick frying pan over a high heat.

Put a tablespoon of the flour in a large bowl and season with plenty of salt and pepper. Add half the liver to the bowl and toss lightly in the flour to coat. Place each slice carefully in the hot fat and cook for 1–2 minutes on each side until lightly browned but not completely cooked through. Transfer to a plate. Toss the remaining liver in the seasoned flour and brown in the pan as before. Transfer to the same plate as the first batch.

Reduce the heat and melt the remaining butter in the same pan. Add the sliced onion and cook for a minute or so, stirring to separate the layers. Next, add the bacon and cook together for 8–10 minutes or until the onion is pale golden brown and the bacon is beginning to crisp. Stir often.

Sprinkle the rest of the flour over the onion and bacon and stir it for a minute or so. Dissolve the stock cube in the just-boiled water and pour slowly into the pan, stirring constantly. Bring to a simmer and cook over a medium heat until the gravy is thickened. Add a dash of tomato ketchup and season with salt and pepper.

Return the liver to the pan with the onion gravy for just 1–2 minutes to warm it through and finish cooking. Serve the liver and bacon with some mash and freshly cooked greens.

KROKETTEN

Mariken van Dolen is from the Netherlands and she showed us some amazing recipes that are her 'taste of home'. Kroketten are a typical Dutch snack. This recipe is for beef kroketten but you can use any type of meat, fish or vegetables in the filling. Preparing kroketten is done in three stages. First you make the stock – depending on the type of kroketten you want to make, you can use chicken, fish, vegetable or beef stock. Next, you prepare the filling or ragout, which must be really thick and firm. Then you make the kroketten.

SERVES 15

STOCK
900g oxtail
100g butter
2 onions, chopped
2 carrots, chopped
1 tbsp salt
2 bay leaves
bouquet garni
6 coriander seeds, crushed (optional)
1 beef stock cube (optional)
salt and pepper

Season the oxtail. Heat the butter in a pan and fry the seasoned oxtail until brown. Add the onions and carrots and continue frying until the onions are nice and brown. Add 2.5–3 litres of water, the tablespoon of salt, bay leaves, bouquet garni and, if using, the crushed coriander seeds. Bring almost to the boil, then turn the gas low, and leave to simmer on the lowest possible heat for a few hours. The longer this cooks, the better it tastes – Mariken normally leaves her stock to cook overnight.

Sieve the (hot) stock through a clean tea towel, then transfer the oxtail bones to a plate and leave them to cool. Make sure you remove all the onion and carrot. Check the seasoning of the stock and add salt or a beef stock cube if you like. Remove the meat from the bones when they are cool and throw away the fat.

RAGOUT
6 gelatine leaves
100g butter
150g flour
1 tsp curry powder
few drops of Worcestershire sauce
1 litre beef stock
oxtail meat

Next make the ragout. Place the gelatine leaves in some water to soak. Melt the butter in a saucepan, but don't let it brown. Add the flour, curry powder and Worcestershire sauce and stir until crumbly. Start adding the stock a ladleful at a time, stirring vigorously after each addition. At first, the mixture will form a smooth ball, but gradually it will become a thick sauce – the mixture has to be really firm and thick to make the kroketten. Add the meat and stir. Then squeeze out the gelatine leaves and stir them in well. Taste the ragout and add more salt, Worcestershire sauce or curry powder as you like. Leave the mixture to cool in the fridge until it is really cold.

FINISHING
4 eggs, beaten
golden breadcrumbs
flour
vegetable oil, for frying

Put the beaten eggs in a low, wide bowl and the breadcrumbs and flour in separate bowls. Take a spoonful of ragout and roll it in your hands into a sausage shape. Roll this in the flour, then the egg and lastly the breadcrumbs, making sure both ends of the kroket are well covered. Place on a plate and continue until all the mixture is used up. Then roll the kroketten in egg and breadcrumbs again.

Heat the oil to 180°C in a deep-fat fryer or large saucepan. Fry the kroketten, a few at a time, until deep brown. If the kroketten start to sizzle, take them out of the pan, as this is a signal that the filling is starting to leak. Serve immediately, but take care – they will be very hot.

You can also freeze the kroketten and fry them straight from the freezer without defrosting. Be sure to freeze them separately so they don't stick together. When cooking frozen kroketten, fry them for about 2 minutes, take them out for 2 minutes, then lower them into the fryer for another 2 minutes until they are deep brown.

You can prepare the kroketten earlier in the day and place them in the fridge to cook when you're ready.

DUTCH PEA SOUP

Another recipe from Mariken, this is traditionally served on very cold winter days alongside the canals when everybody is out skating at the so-called Koek and Zopie (cookie and drink) stands. The soup warms you up and gives you energy. Many mums also serve this soup on Saturdays with fried bread cubes. It's essential to use meat on the bone for flavour.

SERVES 6–8

1kg dried green peas or split peas (or half of each)
1kg pork shank or leg (on the bone)
2 pigs' ears (optional)
200g smoked bacon, cut into cubes
2–3 leeks, sliced
5–7 carrots, sliced
1 celeriac, peeled and cut into cubes
1 head of celery
3 bay leaves
1 bunch of flat-leaf parsley, tied with string
1 smoked sausage, sliced
1 tbsp chopped parsley
salt
pepper

Place the dried green peas and/or split peas in water and soak them as directed on the packet.

Put the pork and the pigs' ears, if using, in a large soup pan with the smoked bacon, leeks, carrots, celeriac, celery, bay leaves, bunch of parsley and salt. Pour in water to come up to about 1–2cm below the rim of the pan and gently bring to the boil. Simmer for a few hours – the longer the better.

Add the soaked peas and the slices of sausage to the soup. Bring everything to the boil again and leave to simmer for another 2–3 hours until the peas are soft. If you want a really thick soup, add only half of the peas and boil the rest separately until soft. Then purée them in a food processor and stir this mixture into the soup.

Remove the pork, ears and parsley. Leave the pork and ears to cool, then remove the meat from the bones and put it back in the soup. Add the fresh chopped parsley and season with salt and pepper.

Serve the soup with dark rye bread and cheese or very thin slices of streaky bacon.

ROCKING ROCK CAKES

**These are often the first cakes kids bring home from school cookery class.
They're scones with attitude really. Rock on!**

MAKES ABOUT 8

225g self-raising flour
100g cold butter, cubed
75g caster sugar,
plus extra for dredging
100g mixed dried fruit
1 medium egg
1 tbsp milk

Preheat the oven to 200°C/Gas 6 and line a baking tray with baking parchment. Sift the flour into a mixing bowl and rub in the butter until the mixture resembles fine breadcrumbs. Stir in the sugar and mixed fruit until everything is well mixed together.

Whisk the egg with the milk and add this to the flour mixture. Stir with a wooden spoon until the mixture comes together in a firmish clump.

Drop rough spoonfuls of the mixture on the baking tray, spacing them well apart as they will spread – you should have about 8. Bake in the centre of the oven for 12–15 minutes until risen and pale golden brown. Dredge the cakes with lots of caster sugar and eat while they're still warm to taste them at their best.

BATTENBURG CAKE

This cake is definitely worth the effort it takes to make and is so much nicer than the shop-bought variety. If you want to make life easier, buy a four-compartment battenburg tin. Works a treat.

SERVES 8

175g softened butter, plus extra for greasing
175g golden caster sugar
3 medium eggs
175g self-raising flour
½ tsp vanilla extract
red food colouring paste

COVERING
6 tbsp apricot jam
500g ready-made marzipan
2–3 tbsp icing sugar, for rolling

The cake batter should have a thick dropping consistency, so make sure you don't over-blend it.

Preheat the oven to 190°C/Gas 5. Grease a 20cm square, loose-based cake tin with butter. Take a 30x 20cm wide strip of baking parchment and make a 5cm fold in the centre. This will create a division in the cake so that the two differently coloured sponges can be cooked at the same time. Line the tin with the baking parchment, keeping the division in the centre.

Put the butter, sugar, eggs, flour and vanilla in a food processor and pulse until well combined. Transfer the batter to a bowl set on scales – it will weigh about 700g. Take half the batter and put it in a different bowl. Add a small dab of red food colouring to one bowl, mixing with the batter until it is pink.

Spoon the cake batters into each side of the prepared tin and smooth the surface with the back of a spoon. Bake in the centre of the oven for about 25 minutes or until the cakes have risen. Cool in the tin for 5 minutes, then slide a knife around the outside of each cake and turn them out onto a wire rack. Leave until cold. If the cakes have risen unevenly, press the surface gently until level.

To assemble the cake, first place one sponge on top of the other and trim off the crusty edges so that the cakes are the same size. Cut the cakes in half to make four long rectangles. Warm the apricot jam in a saucepan until soft, then press through a sieve. Brush the long side of one of the cakes with jam and sandwich together with a cake of a contrasting colour. Do the same with the other cakes. Brush the top of the first cakes with jam and place the cakes on top like a checker board. Brush the top and sides with jam.

Place the marzipan on a surface dusted with icing sugar and roll into a rectangle of about 35 x 25cm and large enough to cover the cake. It should be 4–5mm thick. Turn the cake upside down on the marzipan and brush the underside of the sponges with jam. Wrap fully in the marzipan, taking care to keep it smooth, especially where the ends meet. Turn back over with the seam underneath and place on a serving plate.

AFRICAN WOMEN'S GROUP

The African Women's Group, based in Rose Hill, Oxford, is a community group for women from all parts of Africa or with African origins. It aims to provide support and friendship to the women, many of whom are refugees or asylum seekers. The group encourages members and their families to get involved in a range of activities, including cooking. They run an African food event once a month and offer a lunch of hot and cold traditional dishes. Here are two recipes that often feature.

FRIED PLANTAIN

Fried plantain is a simple but delicious African dish. It's easy and quick to prepare, yet very nutritious.

SERVES 4

2 ripe plantains
salt and chilli pepper (optional)
250ml vegetable oil

Peel the plantains and cut them into discs or diagonal slices of about 0.5–1cm thick. Sprinkle with salt and chilli pepper if desired. Heat the oil in a large pan. Add the plantain discs in batches and fry until golden brown. Drain on kitchen paper and serve hot.

JOLLOF RICE

There are lots of versions of this popular African rice dish. The basis is rice, tomato and onion, but you can add other vegetables, chicken or meat if you like.

SERVES 4

1 tbsp olive or vegetable oil
2 large onions, sliced
2 x 400g cans of plum tomatoes
4 fresh tomatoes, chopped
1 red pepper, diced
85g tomato paste
1/4 tsp cayenne pepper or chilli powder
1 tsp curry powder
1 bay leaf
sprig of thyme
1 stock cube
225g long-grain or basmati rice
salt and black pepper

Heat the oil in a large pan and cook the onions over a gentle heat until translucent. Stir in the canned tomatoes, fresh tomatoes, red pepper and tomato paste, then season with salt, black pepper and cayenne or chilli. Add the curry powder, bay leaf and thyme, then pour in 550ml of water and crumble in the stock cube. Cover and bring to the boil, then reduce the heat and simmer for 20–30 minutes.

Rinse the rice well to remove excess starch, then add it to the tomato mixture. Bring to the boil, then reduce the heat to low. Cover and simmer for 25–30 minutes until the rice is cooked. Check the seasoning before serving.

Continued on page 2

Lazy
weekends

BRAISED STEAKS
WITH GRAVY

This is a real weekend treat. It takes a while to cook but it's worth it, we promise. Serve with some crispy home-made chips – everyone loves a bit of gravy with their chips.

SERVES 4

4 braising steaks, each around 200g
3 tbsp sunflower oil
1 medium onion, halved and cut into 12 wedges
1 garlic clove, crushed
500ml beef stock made with 1 beef stock cube or a 500ml tub of fresh beef stock
1 tbsp tomato purée
4–5 sprigs of fresh thyme or ½ tsp dried thyme
1 bay leaf
1 tsp cornflour
½ tsp English mustard powder
sea salt flakes
freshly ground black pepper

Preheat the oven to 160°C/Gas 3. Trim off any hard fat from the beef and season on both sides with salt and lots of freshly ground black pepper. Heat a tablespoon of the oil in a large non-stick frying pan.

Fry the steaks, 2 at a time, over a medium-high heat for a couple of minutes on each side or until nicely browned. Transfer to a large flameproof casserole dish. Add a little more oil to the pan between batches.

Return the pan to the hob and reduce the heat. Add the remaining oil and gently fry the onion for 5 minutes or until softened and lightly browned, stirring regularly. Stir in the garlic for the last minute of the cooking time.

Transfer the onion and garlic to the casserole, pour over the stock and add the tomato purée. Strip the thyme leaves from the stalks and scatter into the pan (or sprinkle over the dried thyme), add the bay leaf and stir well. Bring to the boil then cover the casserole and transfer carefully to the oven. Cook for 1¼ –1½ hours or until the beef is very tender.

Mix the cornflour and mustard powder in a small bowl and stir in a tablespoon of cold water until smooth. Remove the lid from the casserole dish and stir in the cornflour mixture. Place the casserole over a medium-high heat and simmer for 2–3 minutes until the gravy reduces and becomes thickened and glossy, stirring regularly. Divide the steaks between four warmed plates and spoon over the gravy. Serve with chips.

OLD-FASHIONED RABBIT STEW

This is a good old traditional British stew, but give it a pastry top and you've got rabbit pie.
Rabbit is a really healthy meat and tastes great too. We reckon we should eat more of it.

SERVES 5–6

3 tbsp plain flour
2 tsp dried thyme (wild if possible) or
2 tbsp finely chopped fresh thyme leaves
1 large farmed rabbit or
2 young wild rabbits, jointed into 8 pieces
15g butter
2–3 tbsp sunflower oil
6 rindless smoked streaky bacon
rashers, cut into 2cm squares
2 medium onions, chopped
500ml dry cider
300ml chicken or vegetable stock
2 bay leaves
350g Chantenay carrots or other small,
fat carrots, peeled
150g frozen peas
sea salt flakes
freshly ground black pepper

Mix the flour, thyme, a good pinch of salt and plenty of freshly ground black pepper in a large freezer bag. Wash the rabbit pieces and pat them dry with kitchen paper. Melt the butter with 1 tablespoon of the oil in a large frying pan.

Put the rabbit portions in the freezer bag, a few at a time, and shake well until evenly coated in the flour. Fry the rabbit, a few pieces at a time, until golden brown all over. Put all the front and rear leg portions in a large flameproof casserole dish. Put the saddle pieces on a plate, cover loosely and set aside. These will need less cooking time, so can be added later on. Preheat the oven to 170°C/Gas 3½.

Add a little more oil to the pan and cook the bacon, stirring regularly, until the fat is browned and beginning to crisp. Tip into the casserole dish with the rabbit pieces. Add a dash more oil to the frying pan and fry the onion for about 5 minutes until lightly browned and beginning to soften. Add to the casserole. Sprinkle the meat with any flour remaining in the freezer bag and stir well.

Pour about half the cider into the frying pan and stir with a wooden spoon to lift any sediment from the bottom. Simmer for a few seconds, then pour into the casserole. Add the rest of the cider and the stock. Stir the bay leaves into the casserole, cover and cook in the centre of the oven for 45 minutes.

Remove the casserole from the oven and add the reserved saddle pieces and the carrots. Turn all the rabbit portions over, ensuring that as much of the meat is covered by liquid as possible – not all of it will be. Return to the oven for a further 1¼–2 hours, depending on the type of rabbit you are using.

When the rabbit is tender, skim off any fat that may have risen to the top with a large spoon. Put the casserole dish on the hob, bring to a fast simmer and cook for 3–5 minutes until the liquid reduces to a slightly thickened, gravy-like consistency. Stir in the frozen peas and simmer for a further 3 minutes until tender. Season to taste and serve.

The cooking time depends on what type of rabbit you are using – farmed rabbits will become tender more quickly than wild. Once you've added the saddles and cooked them for an hour, keep checking every 30 minutes or so. Poke the leg portions and the saddle pieces with a knife and if it doesn't slide in easily, return the casserole to the oven.

JEAN'S CHICKEN PIE

Elaine Wilson remembers her mum Jean making this pie for family dinners and celebrations when she was a child and says it's the best – she's never met anyone who didn't love it. We certainly did.

SERVES AT LEAST 8

FILLING
1 medium chicken
1 onion, peeled
6 cloves
1 carrot, peeled
2 bay leaves
1 chicken stock cube
6–8 peppercorns

SHORTCRUST PASTRY
450g plain flour
½ tsp salt or to taste
120g butter, cold
120g white vegetable fat, cold
beaten egg, for glazing

SAUCE
250ml whole milk
55g butter
55g plain flour

Rinse the chicken in cold water and place it in a large pan. Stud the onion with cloves and add it to the pan with the carrot, bay leaves, stock cube and peppercorns. Cover with cold water and bring to the boil, then reduce the heat and simmer until the chicken is cooked. This will take about 45 minutes–1¼ hours, depending on the size of the chicken.

Meanwhile, make the pastry. Sift the flour and salt together into a large mixing bowl. Dice the cold butter and white fat and rub them into the flour until the mixture resembles fine breadcrumbs. Mix in just enough cold water to form a stiff paste. Turn this out onto a lightly floured surface and knead gently to form a smooth ball of dough. Wrap in clingfilm or place in a plastic bag and chill for at least 30 minutes.

When the chicken is cooked, take the pan off the heat. Remove the chicken and place it on a plate. Put the pan back on the heat and reduce the cooking liquid to about 250ml. Pour it into a jug and leave to cool, then skim off the fat and discard it. Put the stock with the onion – cloves removed – into a blender and blitz. Add milk to make the stock up to 500ml.

When the chicken is cool enough to handle, cut the meat into chunks and discard the skin and bones. Melt the butter in a pan and stir in the flour. Gradually add the stock and milk, then bring to the boil, stirring continuously. Reduce the heat and simmer for a minute or two to cook the flour. Taste and adjust the seasoning, then fold the meat gently into the sauce without breaking up the pieces. Set the mixture aside to cool.

Preheat the oven to 220°C/Gas 7. Roll out two-thirds of the pastry and use it to line a 20–25cm pie plate. Add the cooled chicken mix. Brush the edges of the pastry with beaten egg, roll out the remaining pastry and cover the pie. Trim off any excess and pinch the edges together to seal. Decorate the pie with leaves made from trimmings and brush with beaten egg. Make a hole in the top of the pie to allow the steam to escape. Bake in the preheated oven for about 45 minutes.

DEVILLED KIDNEYS

This makes a great snack or quick supper. It's rich and we find a little goes a long way, but boy it's good.

SERVES 4

375g lambs' kidneys (6 kidneys),
skinned if needed
2 tbsp plain flour
25g butter
1 medium onion, finely sliced
1 tbsp tomato purée
1 tbsp English mustard
1–2 tbsp Worcestershire sauce
4 thick slices of crusty bread
butter for spreading
small bunch of fresh parsley, chopped
(optional)
sea salt flakes
freshly ground pepper

Rinse the kidneys under cold running water and pat them dry with kitchen paper. Using scissors, carefully cut the white cores out of the kidneys and discard them. Put the kidneys on a board and cut them into chunky pieces. Tip the flour into a freezer bag and season well with salt and pepper. Add the kidneys and toss them until well coated with the flour.

Melt the butter in a large non-stick frying pan. Add the onion and fry gently for 3–4 minutes or until soft and slightly golden, stirring regularly. Shake off any excess flour from the kidneys and add them to the pan. Cook them with the onion over a medium-high heat for 2–3 minutes until golden, turning every now and then.

Spoon the tomato purée and mustard into the frying pan, then gradually add 300ml of water, stirring constantly. Bring to the boil, add a tablespoon of the Worcestershire sauce to the pan and season with salt and pepper. Reduce the heat and simmer gently for 15 minutes, or until the kidneys are tender and the sauce is thickened, stirring occasionally. Add a little more Worcestershire sauce to taste if you like.

While the kidneys are cooking, toast the bread on both sides until golden, then spread with butter and put on four small plates. Spoon the kidneys and sauce over the buttered toast and scatter with freshly chopped parsley, if using. Serve immediately while piping hot.

Everything depends on taking the time to core the kidneys properly. Dave uses a pair of hairdressing scissors, but any sharp scissors will do the trick.

CHOLENT

This recipe is from Rosalyn Alexander and this is what she told us. 'Cholent is usually prepared before the Jewish Sabbath, so was cooked overnight on a very low heat and served for lunch and dinner the next day. In the old days, Jewish mothers would take the dish to the local baker and leave the pots to cook in their ovens overnight, then bring them home the next day. My mother often made this dish and I remember waking up on Saturday mornings and inhaling the great scent! Before putting the lid on, mum would cover the ingredients with paper and tie it with string and there seemed to be a ceremony of uncovering the paper and seeing how the dish looked. When I was older and went out on a Saturday night, I would come home, take the pot out of the oven and enjoy the last scrapings of cholent.'

SERVES 6

170g butter beans
280g barley
goose fat or sunflower oil
1.5kg beef (brisket or braising steak)
1.8kg potatoes (King Edward or Maris Piper), peeled and left whole

DUMPLING
280g flour
2 tsp baking powder
1 large onion, cut into small cubes
2 tbsp sunflower oil
salt and pepper

Soak the butter beans in cold water for 24 hours before they are needed. You can use canned beans but dried beans give a much better flavour.

On the evening of cooking the dish, first make the dumpling. Put the flour and baking powder in a bowl and add the onion, oil and seasoning. Add enough water to make a soft dough, then chill in the fridge for at least 30 minutes.

Preheat the oven to 120°C/Gas ½. Wash and drain the barley and drain the soaked butter beans. Grease a large heavy casserole dish or a heavy pot with some goose fat or sunflower oil (not olive oil) and place the beef in the middle of the dish. Position the dumpling, beans, barley and potatoes around the beef, then pour in boiling water to cover everything. Season with salt and pepper and cover with a double sheet of baking parchment. Secure by twisting the paper all round under the rim of the dish. Place on a low shelf in the oven and leave to cook overnight.

In the morning, pull the paper aside carefully and take a peek There's usually enough liquid to leave the dish cooking as it is, but if it looks dry, add a little more. You can eat this dish for lunch or anytime afterwards. It becomes darker coloured the longer it's cooked, but if you want it a darker colour for lunch, you could turn the oven heat up a couple of hours before you eat it.

PLAVA CAKE

This is what Rosalyn told us about this recipe. 'My mother could make, bake and have this cake on the table in under an hour. My mother's plava was famous in our family – no one could make it as well as she did – but over the years, I believe I have perfected the recipe. I still use the tin my mother used. It must be almost as old as me, perhaps older!'

SERVES 8–10

3 large eggs
170g caster sugar, plus an extra tablespoon
1 large tbsp sunflower oil, plus extra for greasing the tin
140g self-raising flour

Grease a 23cm cake tin with oil, then sprinkle it with the tablespoon of caster sugar. Preheat the oven to 180°C/Gas 4.

Beat the eggs with the sugar until very pale and thick, then mix in the sunflower oil. Sift the flour and fold it into the mixture with a large metal spoon. Pour the mixture into the prepared tin and bake for about 35 minutes or until spongy to the touch.

When the plava is done, remove it from the oven and leave it to cool in the tin for about 10 minutes before turning it out onto a wire rack.

Rosalyn always uses a bundt-style tin with a hole in the middle, but don't worry if you don't have one. Use a regular tin and the cake will still taste good.

ROAST BELLY OF PORK
WITH APPLES & SAGE

This recipe is brilliant! Enough said.

SERVES 4–5

1.5kg pork belly, deeply scored
2 tbsp finely chopped fresh thyme leaves
2 tsp sea salt flakes
1 tsp coarsely ground black pepper, plus
extra to season
3 medium apples, peeled, quartered,
cored and cut into thick slices
2 medium onions, sliced
good handful of fresh sage leaves
2 tsp plain flour
200ml cider
freshly ground black pepper

Preheat the oven to 240°C/Gas 9. Place the pork on a board and pat the rind dry with kitchen paper if it feels at all damp. Mix the thyme with the salt and pepper and rub this seasoning mixture into the pork rind and the underside of the pork.

Place the pork in a sturdy roasting tin or flameproof baking tray and roast for 25–30 minutes. This will give the rind a chance to bubble and become really crisp. Turn the oven down to 180°C/Gas 4 and continue roasting for another hour.

Toss the apples with the onions, whole sage leaves and a few twists of black pepper. Make a compact pile in the centre of a clean, smallish roasting tin. When ready, remove the pork from the oven and place it on top of the apples and onions, keeping the apple and onion pieces snugly underneath the meat so they don't burn. Keep the first roasting tin to one side because you'll need the cooking juices to make the gravy. Return the pork to the oven and cook for a further hour until the meat is really succulent and tender.

Take the first roasting tin, skim off any fat from the cooking juices and place the tin over a medium heat. Stir in the flour and cook for a minute or so, stirring constantly. Gradually stir in the cider and 100ml of water and bring to a simmer. Cook for 3–4 minutes, while stirring. Strain through a sieve into a small saucepan and season to taste. Set aside.

When the pork is cooked, transfer it to a carving board. Scoop up the apple and onion with a large spoon and place in a warmed serving bowl. Reheat the cider gravy until bubbling and cut the pork into thick slices. Serve the pork and crackling with the apple and sage and the hot gravy.

SPICED TEACAKES

Spiced teacakes before a roaring fire – who could ask for anything more?
And don't forget, teacakes are for life, not just Sundays.

MAKES 6

375g strong white flour,
plus extra for kneading
½ tsp sea salt flakes, lightly crushed
1 x 7g sachet of fast-action dried yeast
1 tsp ground mixed spice
1 tsp ground cinnamon
1 tsp freshly grated nutmeg
finely grated zest of ½ well-scrubbed orange
50g caster sugar
50g butter, cubed
150ml semi-skimmed milk
1 large free-range egg, beaten
125g luxury mixed dried fruit
2 tsp sunflower oil, for greasing
butter, for serving

Mix the flour, salt, yeast, spices, orange zest and sugar in a large bowl. Put the butter and milk in a small saucepan and heat very gently until the butter is melted and the milk is just lukewarm. Remove from the heat and whisk in the egg. Make a well in the centre of the flour mixture and pour in the warm butter, milk and egg. Stir with a wooden spoon until the mixture forms a ball.

Turn out on a very lightly floured surface and knead for 5 minutes to form a smooth, pliable dough. Knead the fruit into the dough for a couple of minutes until evenly distributed. Place the dough in a lightly greased bowl, cover loosely with oiled clingfilm and leave to rise in a warm place for 1½ hours, or until doubled in size and spongy to touch.

Knead the dough lightly and divide into 6 portions. Roll into balls. Using a rolling pin, flatten each ball to a circle around 1cm thick and place on a large baking tray lined with baking parchment. Cover with oiled clingfilm and leave to rise for a further 45 minutes.

Preheat the oven to 190°C/Gas 5. Remove the clingfilm and bake the teacakes in the centre of the oven for 15–18 minutes until well risen and golden brown. Serve warm or leave to cool on a wire rack, then toast. Cut in half when cold using a serrated knife. Grill cut side up until lightly toasted and spread thickly with butter. Eat within 24 hours to enjoy them at their best.

RACLETTE

Jenny Eigenheer and her Swiss husband both love cooking and this Swiss classic is one of their favourites. The melted cheese is prepared with a raclette machine and served with hot new potatoes and salads and pickled vegetables. Suitable cheeses include Raclette, Fontal and Bagnes, available in supermarkets, delis and cheese shops. As a general rule, allow 200g cheese per person.

SERVES 4–6

1kg Raclette cheese or Fontal or Bagnes
black pepper
cayenne pepper

ACCOMPANIMENTS

1kg new potatoes, boiled or steamed in their skins and kept warm
500g carrot salad (see below)
500g celeriac salad (see below)
cornichons
silverskin pickled onions
pickled mushrooms

The preparation of the cheese depends on what sort of machine you have. For round machines with individual trays, cut the cheese into squares of about 6cm. If using a big machine, mount half a cheese into the stand.

Diners should help themselves to a potato and to salads and pickles while they wait for their portion of cheese to melt. Some ham or salami is good, too. Once the cheese is melted, scrape it over the potato and add pepper or cayenne pepper if required. Keep going until you are full!

CARROT SALAD

SERVES 4–6

500g carrots
1 garlic clove, finely chopped
1 red onion, chopped
1 tbsp chopped flat-leaf parsley

SALAD DRESSING

4 tbsp light olive oil or sunflower oil
1 tbsp wine vinegar
1 tsp Dijon mustard
1 tbsp mayonnaise, cream or crème fraîche
dash of Maggi seasoning (optional)
salt

Peel and grate the carrots and mix with the salad dressing. Add garlic, parsley and as much or little red onion as you like.

To make the dressing, simply mix everything together. You can also add minced garlic or red onion and chopped herbs, such as parsley, chives or coriander, if you like. Jenny suggests making up the basic sauce in a screw-topped jar without the mayo or cream and keeping this in the fridge to use as needed.

CELERIAC SALAD

Use 1 celeriac instead of the carrots. Peel and grate the celeriac and mix it with the salad dressing as above. Add garlic, chopped chives and as much or little red onion as you like.

ROAST CHICKEN
WITH MOREL MUSHROOM SAUCE

Jenny's mother-in-law used to make this dish, and Jenny's husband remembers foraging in the woods for morels when he was a child. It's still a regular for family get-togethers.

SERVES 4

1 x 1kg roasting chicken
50g butter or 2 tbsp olive or sunflower oil
3–4 smoked bacon rashers (optional)
salt and pepper

SAUCE

1 x 20g packet of dried morel mushrooms, soaked overnight in 500ml whole milk
30g butter
1 tbsp plain flour
100ml dry white wine
100ml double cream
salt and pepper

Don't be tempted to skip soaking the mushrooms – it's really worth it and the flavoured milk makes the sauce taste so good.

Preheat the oven to 180°C/Gas 4. Rub the chicken with butter or oil and season with salt and pepper. Place the bacon rashers over the breast if using. Place the chicken in a roasting tin and roast for 1–1½ hours. The juices should run clear when you prick the bird between the thigh and breast.

About halfway through the cooking time for the chicken, make the sauce. Drain the soaked mushrooms through a sieve lined with muslin or other clean fine-meshed cloth to remove any sand or grit. Set the mushroomy milk aside. Wash the mushrooms carefully to remove any sand or grit and cut them into bite-sized pieces.

Melt the butter in a pan and add the flour, stirring it in well. Gradually add the wine to make a sauce, stirring all the time and taking care not to let the sauce burn. Add the mushroomy milk to the sauce very slowly so it doesn't curdle. Then add the mushrooms and cook for about 20 minutes. Season with salt and pepper to taste, then add the double cream and heat through gently. Taste and adjust the seasoning if necessary. The sauce should have the consistency of custard.

Carve the chicken and place it on a serving platter. Pour over the juices from the roasting pan and serve with the morel sauce. This is good with rice, pasta or French fries and some vegetables or salad.

COFFEE & WALNUT SPONGE

A deliciously moist, old-fashioned coffee and walnut cake is one of our very favourite treats and we like to make it with Camp chicory and coffee essence. If you can't track this down in your local stores, use very strong black coffee instead. Make sure the walnuts you use are nice and fresh.

SERVES 12

65g walnut halves
225g softened butter, cubed, plus extra for greasing
225g caster sugar
4 medium eggs
225g self-raising flour
1 tsp baking powder
2 tbsp Camp chicory and coffee essence

ICING
150g softened butter, cubed
300g icing sugar, sifted
4 tsp Camp chicory and coffee essence
12 walnut halves

Preheat the oven to 190°C/Gas 5. Butter two 20cm loose-based sandwich tins and line the bases with discs of baking parchment. Put the walnut halves in a food processor and blitz them into fairly fine crumbs, but don't worry if there are a few larger pieces remaining. Tip the walnuts into a bowl.

Put the butter, sugar, eggs, flour, baking powder and coffee essence in a food processor and blend on the pulse setting until well combined and creamy. You may need to remove the lid once or twice and push the mixture down with a rubber spatula. Take care not to process for too long or you will end up with a heavy sponge. Add the blitzed walnuts to the batter and mix until just combined. If you don't have a food processor, finely chop the nuts, tip all the ingredients into a large mixing bowl, then beat like hell!

Spoon the mixture evenly into the greased and lined tins and smooth the surface. Bake on the same shelf in the centre of the oven for about 25 minutes or until the sponge is well risen and just beginning to shrink back from the sides of the tin.

Remove the tins from the oven and leave to cool for 5 minutes before running a knife around the edge of the cakes and turning them out onto a wire rack. Peel off the baking parchment and leave to cool completely.

To make the icing, put the butter in a food processor, or mixing bowl, then add the icing sugar and coffee essence. Blend until the icing is smooth and creamy. Add a little more coffee essence to taste if you like.

Place one of the sponges on a plate or cake stand and spread with half the coffee icing. Add the second sponge and spread the remaining icing over the top. Use the back of a spoon or a rubber spatula to create soft swirls and peaks. Decorate with the walnut halves. Leave to stand for at least an hour before serving if possible to allow the icing to become a little firmer.

GROWING TOGETHER

St George's Community Hub, based in Newtown, Birmingham, is in a multicultural neighbourhood with wonderful spicy cooking traditions from the Caribbean, Angola, Somalia and other parts of the world. The Hub's Growing Together project works with local young people and their parents, grandparents and neighbours to grow organic vegetables, herbs and tropical greenhouse crops. Families then take turns to cook their favourite traditional recipes. Centre director Dr Bob Tyler says it has really brought the community together.

PUMPKIN SOUP

This recipe, given to us by the Growing Together project, comes from the tiny island of Carriacou, off the coast of Grenada. It includes classic Caribbean flavours, such as local ginger, chillies and coconut milk.

SERVES 4–6

½ large pumpkin (preferably organic)
1 large white onion, chopped
2.5cm piece of root ginger, finely chopped
2 garlic cloves, finely chopped
½ Scotch bonnet chilli, deseeded and chopped
4–5 sprigs of thyme
1 x 400ml can of coconut milk
salt

Cut the pumpkin in half, then into wedges. Peel and deseed each wedge and cut the pumpkin flesh into cubes of about 2.5cm square.

Put the pumpkin cubes in a pan with the onion, ginger, garlic and chilli. Strip the leaves from the thyme and add those in too. Pour in about 400ml of water, bring to the boil and cook until the pumpkin has turned to a pulp.

Pour in the coconut milk and season to taste with salt, then reduce the heat and leave the soup to simmer for another 5–10 minutes. If you like, add chunks of breadfruit or sweet potato towards the end of the cooking process.

High tea

EGG & BACON PIE

We just can't get enough of this, particularly when made with maple-cured streaky bacon.
Add a couple of sliced sausages and you've got an all-day breakfast pie.

SERVES 4

FILLING
1 tbsp sunflower oil
8–10 smoked streaky bacon rashers
9 large eggs
4 tbsp whole milk
sea salt flakes
freshly ground black pepper

PASTRY
300g plain flour, plus extra for dusting
good pinch of sea salt flakes
175g butter, chilled and cubed
1 large egg

To make the filling, heat the oil in a large non-stick frying pan. Cut the bacon rashers in half through the middle and add them to the pan. Fry over a medium heat for 4–5 minutes until the fat is golden and crisp, turning them once. Remove the bacon from the heat and leave to cool. Place a sturdy baking tray in the oven and preheat to 190°C/Gas 5.

For the pastry, put the flour in a food processor and add the salt, crumbling it as you do so. Add the butter and blitz on the pulse setting until the mixture resembles fine breadcrumbs. Whisk the egg with a tablespoon of cold water and pour onto the flour and butter mixture with the motor running. Continue blending until the dough begins to form a ball.

Turn the pastry out onto a lightly floured board. Knead quickly into a ball and cut in half. Roll out one half until it is about 5mm thick and line a 23cm pie plate, leaving any excess pastry overhanging the edge. Scatter the bacon loosely over the pastry case. Gently break 6 of the eggs into the pastry case, spaced evenly apart between the bacon rashers. Beat the remaining eggs with the milk and plenty of salt and pepper.

Slowly pour the beaten eggs into the pastry case, stopping every now and then to allow the beaten egg to find its way between the whole eggs and the bacon. Leave 2–3 tablespoons of the mixture in the bowl for glazing the top of the pie.

Roll out the rest of the pastry to make a lid for the pie. Brush the edge of the pastry case with beaten egg and milk and gently lift the pastry lid over the filling. Press the edges firmly to seal, then trim. Use a fork to help seal the edge all the way around the pie. Brush with the remaining beaten egg to glaze.

Bake the pie on the preheated baking tray for 45–55 minutes until pale golden brown and cooked through. Test by piercing the centre with a sharp knife – the filling should be just set. If it's still runny, put the pie back in the oven for a few minutes. Leave to stand for at least 15 minutes before serving.

This pie needs plenty of salt and pepper so don't skimp on the seasoning. Serve warm or at room temperature to taste it at its best.

CORNED BEEF & ONION PIE

You can make your own shortcrust pastry for this tasty pie or buy a block of ready-made. Our pastry is rich, short and very tasty. If you have problems rolling it, don't worry, just patch up any gaps and carry on. This is great served hot with baked beans or gravy and it's also delicious cold.

SERVES 6

FILLING
15g butter
1 tbsp sunflower oil
1 large onion, sliced or chopped
2 celery sticks, trimmed, de-stringed and sliced
2 medium carrots, cut into roughly 1cm dice
300g potatoes, preferably Maris Pipers, peeled and cut into roughly 1cm dice
good squirt of tomato ketchup (1–2 tbsp)
1 x 340g can of corned beef
freshly ground black pepper

PASTRY
300g plain flour, plus extra for rolling
good pinch of sea salt
175g cold butter, cubed
1 large egg

For the filling, melt the butter with the oil in a large non-stick frying pan. Add the onion, celery, carrots and potatoes. Cook over a low heat for about 15 minutes until the vegetables are softened and beginning to colour, stirring regularly. The carrots should retain a little 'bite'.

Add the ketchup and stir into the vegetables for a few seconds before adding the corned beef. Break the beef into chunky pieces with a wooden spoon and mix with the vegetables. Season with pepper – you shouldn't need salt as the corned beef is fairly salty anyway – and remove from the heat. Leave to cool for about 20 minutes.

Preheat the oven to 190°C/Gas 5. To make the pastry, put the flour, salt and butter in a food processor and blitz on the pulse setting until the mixture resembles breadcrumbs. Lightly whisk the egg with a tablespoon of cold water in a small bowl. Slowly pour all but 1 tablespoon of the egg mixture into the food processor with the motor running and blend until the mixture begins to form a ball.

Turn the pastry out onto a well-floured work surface and bring it together into a ball. Take about a third of the pastry, roll it out and use it to line a 23cm pie plate or 20cm round ceramic quiche dish or deep Victoria sandwich tin. Leave any excess pastry overhanging the edge. Brush the pastry edge lightly with the reserved egg.

Spoon the filling into the pastry base and spread to all the sides. Flour the surface once more and roll out the remaining pastry. Lift the rolled pastry over the rolling pin and place gently over the filling. Press the edges firmly together then trim neatly. Press a fork around the edge to seal.

Brush the top of the pastry with the egg, cut a cross in the centre and place on a baking tray. Bake for about 40 minutes or until the pastry is golden brown and the filling piping hot.

BEEF & HONEY STEW

Polly Findlay and her husband are farmers in Yorkshire and they like to cook with produce from their farm, including their own honey. This is one of Polly's favourite recipes.

SERVES 4

30g plain flour
450g stewing steak, cut into 2.5cm cubes
oil, for frying
1 onion
2 carrots
2 leeks
½ turnip
1 tbsp honey
550ml beef stock
2 large potatoes
salt and pepper to taste

Put the flour in a freezer bag, then add the cubes of meat and shake well to coat. Heat the oil in a large pan and brown the meat a few pieces at a time – adding too much meat at once makes the meat steam rather than brown. Set the meat aside as it is browned.

Cut the vegetables into similar-sized pieces. Fry the onion in the same pan you used for the meat, adding more oil if needed. Once the onion is browned, add all the other ingredients except the potatoes. Put a lid on the pan and simmer the stew for at least 2 hours – the longer it cooks, the better it will be.

Twenty minutes before serving, add the chunks of potato to the stew – adding them at this point means they keep their shape. Season to taste before serving.

WELSH RAREBIT

Cheese on toast, by any other name. When you're cold, tired and hungry, nothing beats it.

SERVES 4

25g butter
25g plain flour
100ml strong, dark beer
50ml whole milk
150g mature Cheddar cheese, grated
1 egg yolk
1 tsp English mustard
4 tsp Worcestershire sauce
good pinch of cayenne pepper (optional)
4 thick slices of wholemeal or granary bread
freshly ground black pepper

Melt the butter in a non-stick saucepan and stir in the flour. Cook over a low heat for about half a minute, while stirring. Slowly add the beer, then the milk. Simmer for 2–3 minutes, stirring constantly until the sauce is thick and smooth.

Add the cheese, egg yolk, mustard, Worcestershire sauce and cayenne pepper, if using. Cook until the cheese melts, stirring constantly. Season with lots of freshly ground black pepper and set aside to cool for a couple of minutes. Leaving the sauce to cool a little will help you spread it more thickly on the toast. Preheat the grill until hot.

Place the bread on a baking tray lined with foil and toast on each side until golden. Spread the cheese sauce thickly over the bread, making sure the slices are completely covered so the edges don't burn. Return to the grill for 20–30 seconds longer until lightly browned and bubbling.

MEATBALLS IN GRAVY

These are top-notch. You don't get them like this in a can.

SERVES 4

250g lean minced beef
250g minced pork
1 small onion, very finely chopped
1 garlic clove, finely chopped
25g fresh white breadcrumbs
2 tsp dried mixed herbs
2 tsp sunflower oil
sea salt flakes
freshly ground black pepper

GRAVY
1 tbsp sunflower oil
1 medium onion, finely sliced
1 tbsp plain flour
150ml red wine
300ml beef stock made with
1 beef stock cube
1 tbsp tomato purée

Put the beef and pork mince in a large bowl and add the onion, garlic, breadcrumbs and dried herbs. Mix well with clean hands, then divide the mixture into 20 portions and roll into small, neat balls.

Heat the 2 teaspoons of sunflower oil in a large non-stick frying pan and fry the meatballs for 6–8 minutes, or until nicely browned on all sides. Roll and turn the meatballs around in the pan as they brown to prevent them from becoming flattened on one side. Transfer them to a large saucepan.

To make the gravy, heat the tablespoon of sunflower oil in the same frying pan and fry the onion over a low heat for 5 minutes until softened, stirring regularly. Sprinkle the flour into the pan and stir well.

Slowly add the red wine and then the stock and tomato purée, stirring constantly. Pour the gravy over the meatballs and bring to the boil. Reduce the heat, cover the pan with a lid and leave to simmer gently over a low heat for 30 minutes, stirring occasionally.

Remove the lid and turn up the heat under the pan. Boil the gravy for another 3–5 minutes or until thickened. Adjust the seasoning to taste. Serve the meatballs and gravy with mashed potatoes and peas.

MEAT PATTIES

We met Lisa Hobson in Leeds and she told us how she'd found a book of handwritten recipes that had belonged to her step-mum. The recipes are just ingredients – no methods – so Lisa has had to work them out for herself. We love these little meat patties.

MAKES 10

1 small onion, chopped
1 tbsp oil or butter
1 thick slice of bread
120g roast beef or other cooked meat
leftover gravy (or make some up with gravy mix)
salt and pepper

PASTRY
75g fat (half lard and half butter)
170g plain flour
pinch of salt
1 egg, beaten with a drop of milk

First make the pastry. Rub the fat into the flour, add the salt and mix with enough water to form a dough – you can do this in a food processor if you prefer. Wrap the dough in clingfilm and leave it to rest in the fridge while you make the filling.

Fry the onion in the oil or butter until soft, then leave to cool. Put the bread in a food processor and blitz to make breadcrumbs. Add the meat and onion and pulse until coarsely chopped. Tip everything into a bowl and add sufficient gravy to make a soft mixture. Season to taste.

Preheat the oven to 200°C/Gas 6. Roll out the pastry and cut 10 large circles for the bases of the pies and 10 smaller circles for the lids.

Place the larger pastry rounds in patty tins and add a heaped teaspoon of filling to each. Dampen the edges of the patties with water and add the lids, making sure the edges are well sealed. Brush the patties with the beaten egg and pierce a hole in each one to allow the steam to escape.

Bake the patties in the preheated oven for 20–30 minutes until golden.

DIGGERS

Two more recipes from Lisa. You can make this flapjack-style treat as cookies or a traybake.
Delicious either way.

MAKES AT LEAST 12 SLICES

120g plain flour
225g caster sugar
100g oats
80g desiccated coconut
120g butter
1 tbsp golden syrup
1 level tsp bicarbonate of soda
2 tbsp boiling water

Preheat the oven to 160°C/Gas 3. Mix the flour, sugar, oats and coconut together in a large mixing bowl. Put the butter in a small pan with the golden syrup and heat gently until melted. Mix the bicarb with 2 tablespoons of boiling water and add this to the butter and syrup mixture. Pour the liquid over the dry ingredients and mix well.

Tip the mixture into a greased square tin and press down. Bake in the preheated oven for 20 minutes or until golden. Alternatively, you can shape the mixture into cookies and place them on a greased baking tray. Cook for 10–15 minutes or until golden.

YORKSHIRE MACAROONS

Lisa's gran used to make these for her family and Lisa loves them too.

MAKES 12–14

2 egg whites
150g caster sugar
225g desiccated coconut
100g good-quality milk chocolate
100g good-quality dark chocolate

Preheat the oven to 180°C/Gas 4. Line a baking tray with greaseproof paper.

Whisk the egg whites and sugar until frothy, then stir in the coconut and mix well. Use an egg cup to shape the mixture into 'domes' and turn these out onto the greaseproof paper. Repeat until all the mixture is used. Bake in the preheated oven for 15–20 minutes or until light golden brown. Remove from the oven and leave them to cool on the baking tray.

When the macaroons are set, melt the chocolates in separate bowls. Dip the macaroons in the chocolate to coat half of each one and place on greaseproof paper to set. Coat some in milk chocolate and some in dark.

ECCLES CAKES

We used to call these dead fly pies when we were lads. They are scrumptious served warm with a cup of tea, or as a quick pud with a good dollop of cream or ice cream. They keep for a couple of days in an airtight container and also warm up beautifully.

MAKES 10–12

plain flour, for rolling
500g ready-made puff pastry
1 egg white
3–4 tbsp caster sugar

FILLING
40g butter
50g light muscovado sugar
100g currants
35g cut mixed peel
heaped ¼ tsp ground mixed spice
finely grated zest of ½ lemon

To make the filling, gently melt the butter in a saucepan and stir in the sugar, currants, mixed peel, spice and lemon zest. Remove from the heat and set aside to cool. Preheat the oven to 200°C/Gas 6.

Dust the work surface with flour and roll out the pastry until it's about 4mm thick. Using a 10cm biscuit cutter, cut the pastry into 10–12 circles. Place a tablespoon of the filling mixture in the centre of each circle.

Beat the egg white until it is slightly frothy. Brush a little beaten egg white around the edge of each pastry circle. One at a time, bring the pastry up around the filling and press the edges together to form little purses. It doesn't matter if they are a little bit wonky as they will be rolled again.

Turn each cake over onto a floured surface and roll into a roughly 8.5cm circle. Place on a baking tray lined with baking parchment and score the surface of each one 3–4 times with a sharp knife.

Brush the cakes with more beaten egg white and sprinkle about half a teaspoon of caster sugar over each one. Bake in the centre of the oven for 18–20 minutes until the cakes are nicely risen and the tops are crisp and golden brown. Cool for a few minutes, then serve warm.

MOM'S HOCKEY PUCK MEATLOAF

American-born Nancy Davis lives in England now but still loves to cook the food she was brought up on. Her mum used to make meatloaf badly and her dad named it 'Mom's hockey puck', as it was so hard it bounced off the floor when dropped! Nancy's version though is yummy, as is her potato salad.

SERVES 4–6

1kg minced steak
1 large red onion, chopped
2 slices of bread, made into crumbs
3 tbsp tomato ketchup
1 medium egg
2 tbsp brown sauce
1 tsp Worcestershire sauce
50–100g Parmesan cheese, grated
1 tbsp fresh oregano
1 tbsp chopped parsley
1 tbsp milk
salt and pepper

Preheat the oven to 180°C/Gas 4. Mix all the ingredients together until the mixture pulls away from the sides of the bowl and forms a ball. Add more breadcrumbs if you need them. Form the mixture into a loaf shape.

Place the mixture in an ovenproof dish or a loaf tin and bake in the centre of the oven for 50–60 minutes until the centre is firm. Great hot or cold, served with potato salad.

POTATO SALAD

SERVES 8

8–10 medium-sized red potatoes
1 tbsp milk
1–2 tbsp American mustard
a few drops of vinegar
2–3 tsp dill pickle juice
½ tsp sugar
mayonnaise, to taste
chopped dill pickle (optional)
1 hard-boiled egg (optional)

Cut each potato into 8 pieces and boil in salted water until tender. Drain and set the potatoes aside to cool slightly.

Mix the milk, mustard, vinegar, pickle juice and sugar together in a small bowl. When the potatoes have cooled, pour over the mixture so the potatoes are coated but not swimming. Add mayonnaise to taste and the pickle and egg if using. Chill in the fridge for a couple of hours before serving.

HOME-MADE LEMON CURD

A perfect lemon curd with just the right amount of zing. Spread thickly on freshly buttered bread or use as a delicious filling for cakes and biscuits.

MAKES 1 JAR

100g caster sugar
finely grated zest of 2 unwaxed lemons
freshly squeezed juice of 3 lemons
2 large whole eggs
2 large egg yolks
75g unsalted butter,
cut into small cubes

Put the sugar in a heatproof bowl and stir in the lemon zest and juice. Whisk in the whole eggs and egg yolks. Drop the butter into the bowl and set over a saucepan of very gently simmering water, making sure the bowl doesn't touch the water itself.

Stir the mixture with a wooden spoon for about 5 minutes until the butter melts. Use a whisk to stir the ingredients and cook for 8–10 minutes more or until the lemon curd is thickened to the consistency of custard and leaves a light trail when the whisk is lifted. It will continue to thicken in the jar, so don't allow it to overheat or the eggs could scramble.

Pour the hot lemon curd into a warm, very clean jar and leave to cool. Cover the curd with a disc of waxed paper or baking parchment and seal with the lid. Keep the lemon curd in the fridge and use within 2 weeks.

Warm the jar in a low oven for a few minutes before using.

LUSCIOUS LEMON SWISS ROLL

This teatime lovely features a light-as-a-feather lemon sponge, filled with lemon icing and home-made lemon curd. If you fancy a more traditional Swiss roll, flavour the sponge with half a teaspoon of vanilla extract and simply fill with raspberry jam and butter icing instead.

SERVES 8

butter, for greasing
3 large eggs
115g caster sugar, plus 4 tbsp
finely grated zest of 1 unwaxed lemon
115g plain flour

LEMON BUTTER ICING
200g icing sugar
125g softened butter
2 tsp freshly squeezed lemon juice
home-made lemon curd
(see page 135)

To check the sponge is cooked, touch the centre. It should spring back immediately.

Grease and line a 33 x 23cm Swiss roll tin with buttered baking parchment. Preheat the oven to 200°C/Gas 6. Put the eggs, 115g of sugar and lemon zest in a heatproof bowl and place over a pan of gently simmering water. Whisk with an electric whisk until the mixture is pale, creamy and thick enough to leave a trail when the whisk is lifted.

Carefully remove the bowl from the heat and continue whisking for a further 5 minutes. Sift over half the flour and, using a large metal spoon, lightly fold it into the egg mixture. Sift over the remaining flour and fold in. It's important to use gentle movements to retain as much air as possible in the batter, but you'll need to watch out for pockets of flour.

Pour the mixture slowly into the prepared tin and gently spread with a spatula, so the base of the tin is evenly covered. Bake for 10–12 minutes until well risen, pale golden brown and firm to the touch.

Place a damp tea towel on the work surface and cover with a sheet of baking parchment. Dredge with the 4 tbsp of sugar – this will help stop the outside of the sponge sticking. Working quickly, turn the cake out onto the sugared paper and carefully remove the lining paper. Using a sharp knife, cut off the crusty edges from the 2 long sides. Roll the Swiss roll from one of the short ends, starting with a tight turn to make a good round shape and keeping the sugared paper inside the roll. Set on a wire rack and leave to cool.

To make the icing, put the icing sugar and butter in a bowl and beat until smooth and creamy. Add the lemon juice and beat again. When the cake is cold, gently unroll but do not flatten it or it could crack. Spread the cake with lemon butter icing to within 1cm of the edges. Spoon the lemon curd on top – you'll need about half the jar – and spread it evenly over the icing. Slowly roll the cake up again, enclosing the filling, and place on a plate. Sprinkle with extra sugar if you like.

LIFT COMMUNITY TRUST

This is a voluntary organisation, set up in 2001 to work with disadvantaged people. Based on a housing estate in Birmingham, Lift aims to support the local community and enable people to play a fuller part in society. Cooking is a key activity at the centre and they have set up a café called the Taste of Haven, which provides home-made Caribbean food to eat there or have delivered to your home.

CHICKEN WITH RICE, PEAS & DUMPLINGS

There are countless versions of this Caribbean meal, but this is how they cook it at the Taste of Haven.

SERVES 6

150g plain flour
½ tsp garlic powder
1 tbsp Hot & Spicy Seasoning
1½ tbsp all-purpose seasoning
1 packet of Hot & Spicy Chicken Coating
6 boneless chicken breasts
sunflower oil, for deep-frying

DUMPLINGS
¼ tsp salt
250g self-raising flour
2–3 tbsp oil

SAUCE
1 onion, chopped
½ red, green and yellow pepper, chopped
1 Scotch bonnet, deseeded and chopped
2 tbsp ketchup
1 tbsp gravy browning
2 tbsp sugar
1 tbsp cornflour
black pepper

RICE & PEAS
1 x 400g can of red kidney beans
1 x 400ml can of coconut milk
1 Scotch bonnet, deseeded and chopped
2 spring onions
1 sprig of thyme
400g long-grain rice

Mix the plain flour with the garlic powder, seasonings and chicken coating in a bowl. Dip the chicken breasts into the mixture until well coated.

Heat the oil in a deep-fat fryer to about 170°C. Fry the chicken, a few pieces at a time, until cooked through and golden brown. Serve with dumplings, sauce and rice and peas.

DUMPLINGS
Stir the salt into the flour. Add water to make a dough and knead together well. Shape the mixture into small balls.

Heat the oil in a frying pan and shallow fry the dumplings for 2–4 minutes until golden.

SAUCE
Bring about 250ml of water to the boil. Add the chopped onion, peppers and Scotch bonnet and boil for 3 minutes. Add the ketchup, gravy browning and sugar, then simmer for another 3 minutes. In a small bowl, mix the cornflour with a tablespoon of water, then stir this into the sauce to thicken. Season with black pepper.

RICE & PEAS
Tip the beans into a pan, add 400ml of water and boil for 3 minutes. Add the other ingredients, except the rice, bring to the boil again and cook for at least 4 minutes. Then add the rice and, if necessary, add a little extra boiling water so that the rice is just covered. Put a lid on the pan and cook for 12–15 minutes until the rice is done. Season to taste.

Distant shores

MULLIGATAWNY SOUP

A delicious curried vegetable soup with rice, mulligatawny can be blended for a smooth soup or left as diced vegetables in a fragrant broth – the choice is yours. If you're planning on blitzing the soup, the vegetables can be cut chunky, but go a bit more delicate for the unblended version. For a more filling meal, add some cooked chicken or mince to the soup and heat through before serving.

SERVES 4–5

25g butter
1 tbsp sunflower oil
1 large onion, chopped fairly small
2 garlic cloves, chopped
2 medium carrots, cut into 1.5cm cubes
2 celery sticks, trimmed, stringed and thinly sliced
1 medium sweet potato, cut into roughly 1.5cm cubes
1 eating apple, peeled, quartered and cut into roughly 1.5cm cubes
1 tbsp medium curry powder
1 litre of stock made with 1 chicken or vegetable stock cube
1 tbsp tomato purée
1 tbsp mango chutney
100g easy-cook long-grain rice
natural yoghurt or soured cream, to serve
fresh coriander or flat-leaf parsley, to garnish (optional)
sea salt flakes
freshly ground black pepper

Melt the butter with the oil in a large saucepan and stir in the onion, garlic, carrots, celery and sweet potato. Cook over a medium heat for 10 minutes, stirring regularly until the vegetables are beginning to soften and lightly brown. Stir in the apple pieces and sprinkle over the curry powder. Cook for 2 minutes more, while stirring.

Pour over the stock and stir in the tomato purée and mango chutney. Bring to the boil, then reduce the heat slightly and leave to simmer for 30 minutes, stirring occasionally until all the vegetables are tender.

While the soup is simmering, half fill a medium pan with water and bring to the boil. Add the rice and return to the boil. Cook for 10 minutes or until tender. Drain the rice in a sieve and rinse under running water until cold.

When the soup is ready, either stir the rice straight into it or allow to cool for a few minutes, then blitz with a stick blender or in a food processor until smooth before stirring in the rice. Add enough water to give a good consistency – 150–200ml should be about right. Heat the rice in the soup for 3–4 minutes until hot and season to taste before serving.

Ladle the soup into deep bowls and top with natural yoghurt or soured cream. Garnish with sprigs of coriander or flat-leaf parsley if you like.

FRESH FRUIT PAVLOVA

This pavlova has a crisp meringue shell around a soft, marshmallowy centre and
is filled with lots of softly whipped cream and heaps of your favourite fresh fruit.
Is it from New Zealand? Is it from Australia? Who cares? It tastes great!

SERVES 6

MERINGUE
4 large egg whites
225g caster sugar
½ tsp vanilla extract
1 tbsp cornflour

FILLING
400ml double cream
400g strawberries, hulled and
halved if large
200g raspberries
150g blueberries
3 passion fruit (optional)
Cape gooseberries (optional)
mint sprigs and sifted icing sugar,
to decorate

Preheat the oven to 150°C/Gas 2. Put the egg whites in a large, grease-free bowl and whisk with an electric whisk until stiff but not dry. They are ready when you can turn the bowl upside down without the eggs sliding out.

Gradually whisk in the sugar, just a tablespoon at a time, whisking for a few seconds between each addition. Adding the sugar slowly will help build up volume in the meringue and make it stiff and shiny. Finally, whisk in the vanilla extract and cornflour until well combined.

Dab a small amount of the meringue in the corners of a large, sturdy baking tray or sheet. Place a 25cm dinner plate on a sheet of baking parchment and draw round it. Turn it over and place the parchment on the baking tray, holding it in place with the dabs of meringue. You should be able to see the circle through the paper.

Spoon the meringue into the circle and shape with the back of a serving spoon or with a rubber spatula to create a large, meringue nest, with soft peaks rising on all sides. Place in the centre of the oven and bake for 1 hour until very lightly coloured and crisp on the outside. (If the meringue seems to be becoming too brown, reduce the temperature of the oven.) Turn the oven off and leave the meringue for a further hour to cool. Remove from the oven and leave to cool completely. Serve within 6–8 hours.

Up to 2 hours before serving, carefully transfer the meringue to a large serving platter or board. Whip the cream until soft peaks form and spoon into the centre of the meringue. Top with the berry fruits. Cut the passion fruit in half, if using, and scrape the pulp over the other fruit. Decorate with sprigs of mint and dust with sifted icing sugar.

If you prefer a more chewy meringue, cook for around 2 hours, turn the oven off and leave to cool for 1 hour in the oven before cooling completely.

CHICKEN & CHORIZO PAELLA

Karen Mulholland lives in Northern Ireland, but she fell in love with Spanish cooking when she first visited the country 20 years ago. Since then, she has perfected her repertoire of Spanish classics.

SERVES 6 OR SO

1–2 tbsp oil
12 chicken pieces (leg or thigh) on the bone
1 cured chorizo sausage
1 large onion, finely chopped
3 garlic cloves, crushed
2 red peppers, sliced
2–3 red chillies, deseeded and chopped
(or use dried chillies to taste)
2 tsp smoked paprika
(use mild or dulce if you don't like hot spices!)
about 1.5 litres chicken stock
about 400g Spanish paella rice
handful of flat-leaf parsley
12 cleaned mussels or clams (optional)

Heat the oil in a large ovenproof pan or paella pan and fry the chicken pieces until nicely browned. Remove them from the pan and set aside.

Slice the chorizo into pieces about the size of a pound coin and fry them until they are crisp and the lovely juice is released into the pan. Add the onion and cook until soft, then the garlic and fry for another 2–3 minutes. Then add the red peppers, chillies and smoked paprika and cook for another 2–3 minutes.

Return the chicken pieces to the pan and pour in the stock. Simmer for 20–25 minutes until the chicken is tender. Add the rice to the pan, cover with a lid and place in the oven at 180°C/ Gas 4 for 30 minutes or until all the liquid has been absorbed and the rice is cooked. Alternatively, if using a paella pan, cover it with foil and continue cooking on the stove over a low heat as the pan probably won't fit in the oven! Sprinkle with parsley before bringing the pan to the table and let everyone dig in.

For an even more authentic dish, add a dozen or so cleaned mussels or clams to the pan for the last 20 minutes of the cooking time. Discard any that don't open.

CATALAN TOMATO BREAD

This is gorgeous with dry white wine or Fino sherry as an appetizer! The salt makes you want to drink more though so be careful! If you're not keen on tomatoes, leave them out – it's just as nice without them.

SERVES 6 OR SO

1 sourdough loaf (or similar dense bread)
3–4 garlic cloves, cut in half
2–3 fresh organic tomatoes, cut in half
extra virgin olive oil
sea salt flakes

Slice the bread and toast the slices on both sides. Then rub one side of each with a cut clove of garlic.

Next, rub the cut side of a tomato onto the garlicky side of each piece of toast to give a nice reddish colour. Arrange the toasts on a serving plate, drizzle them with olive oil and sprinkle with sea salt.

CHICKEN CHASSEUR

Throw away those jars of instant chasseur sauce and discover the real thing. This is a simple, classic recipe for chicken chasseur – or hunter's chicken – and makes a tasty supper on a winter's evening.

SERVES 4

3 tbsp plain flour
8 chicken thighs, skin on
3 tbsp mild olive oil or sunflower oil
3 banana (long) shallots, finely chopped,
plus 3 banana (long) shallots, quartered lengthways (6 shallots in total)
3–4 sprigs of fresh thyme or 1 tsp dried thyme
2 bay leaves
2 garlic cloves, finely chopped
300ml dry white wine
500ml chicken stock (fresh or made with a good-quality chicken stock cube)
2 tbsp tomato purée
150g chestnut mushrooms, wiped and halved
sea salt flakes
freshly ground black pepper

Put the flour in a large freezer bag and season it well with sea salt and black pepper. Drop the chicken thighs, 4 at a time, into the seasoned flour and shake them well until they are all lightly coated.

Heat 1 tablespoon of the oil in a large non-stick frying pan. Place the chicken thighs in the pan, skin-side down, and cook them over a medium-high heat for 4–5 minutes until golden brown. Turn over and cook on the other side for a further 2 minutes until golden. Transfer to a large flameproof casserole dish or saucepan.

Using the same frying pan, heat a second tablespoon of the oil and add all the shallots, a few sprigs of thyme, or the dried thyme, and the bay leaves. Fry over a medium heat for 5 minutes until soft, stirring regularly. Add the garlic and fry for a further 2–3 minutes until softened.

Tip the shallots, garlic and herbs into the pan with the chicken. Pour over the white wine and bring to the boil. Simmer for a few seconds, then add the chicken stock, tomato purée and plenty of seasoning and stir lightly. Bring to a gentle simmer and cook uncovered for 20 minutes – spoon off any fat that rises to the surface.

Meanwhile, wipe out the frying pan used to fry the shallots with a wad of kitchen paper. Place over a medium-high heat, add the remaining tablespoon of olive oil and fry the mushrooms for 2–3 minutes until lightly browned. Set them aside.

Once the chicken has been simmering for 20 minutes, stir in the mushrooms. Cook for a further 15 minutes, until the chicken is tender and the sauce is glossy and has reduced enough to lightly coat the back of a spoon. Adjust the seasoning to taste and serve.

Look out for long, banana, shallots as they make all the difference to the appearance of this dish. If you can't get hold of any, use 8 traditional shallots or 4 small onions instead. Chop half of them finely and cut the rest into halves or quarters, depending on size. If you avoid cutting through the root ends, the layers will stay together much better.

ESCABECHE OF PARTRIDGE

Conolly McCausland is a reminder that sometimes dads know best too! Conolly's mum is from Argentina and Conolly likes to cook dishes he has learned from her. In Argentina, the escabeche cooking method is used as a way of preserving meat or fish – escabeche means pickled in Spanish.

SERVES 5

5 partridges, cleaned
2 onions, chopped
4 carrots, cut into fine slices or matchsticks
1 tsp black peppercorns
3 bay leaves
4 garlic cloves, peeled
125ml white wine vinegar
75ml white wine
240ml olive or corn oil
4 slices of lemon
1 tbsp chopped flat-leaf parsley
salt and pepper

Put the partridges in a large, flameproof casserole dish. Add the onions, carrots, peppercorns, bay leaves, garlic, vinegar, wine and oil. Season with a pinch of salt.

Cover the casserole with a lid and simmer gently on top of the stove until the birds are cooked – this should take about 40 minutes. Ten minutes before they are due to be ready, add the slices of lemon.

Remove the pan from the heat, and leave the birds to cool in the liquid. Once the partridges are cold, carve them and serve with the escabeche vegetables, having removed the bay leaves and lemon slices. Sprinkle with parsley and pour over some of cooking liquid. Serve with crusty fresh bread to mop up juices.

EMPANADAS

The perfect portable meal – Argentinian style – and another of Conolly's favourites. If you don't want to make your own pastry, you can buy ready-made empanada wrappers in some delis or from Argentinian food suppliers on the internet. The quantity of pastry here is enough for about 12 empanadas.

MAKES ABOUT 12

EMPANADA PASTRY
450g plain flour
2 tsp baking powder
1 tsp salt
60g butter, diced
60g lard, diced

CRIOLLAS (MEAT FILLING)
2 tbsp olive oil
1 onion, finely chopped
1 green pepper, finely chopped
400g best beef, such as silverside or lean stewing beef, minced
1 tsp paprika
1 tsp chilli powder
30g raisins
12 green olives, pitted and chopped
2 hard-boiled eggs, chopped
1 tsp cumin
good pinch of salt
vegetable oil, for frying
1 tsp caster sugar

CHOCLO (SWEETCORN FILLING)
100g butter
3 spring onions, finely chopped
½ green pepper, finely chopped
1 x 340g can of choclo (sweetcorn)
about 250ml béchamel sauce
handful of chopped parsley
2 tbsp grated Parmesan cheese
pinch of chilli or cayenne pepper
1 tsp caster sugar

Mix the flour, baking and salt in a bowl. Add the diced butter and lard and rub them into the flour with your fingertips until the mixture has the texture of fine breadcrumbs. Add enough cold water to form a soft dough. Put the dough in the fridge to rest for about an hour.

CRIOLLAS (MEAT FILLING)

Heat the oil in a frying pan, add the onion and fry until it is transparent. Add the green pepper and meat and sauté until the meat has browned, then add the paprika and chilli powder. Take the pan off the heat and add the raisins, olives, eggs, cumin and salt.

Roll out the pastry and cut out circles using a coffee saucer or a wine glass, depending on how big you want the empanadas. Put a small spoonful of filling onto one half of a pastry circle – not too much. Wet the edges of the pastry with a little water, fold the pastry over the filling and pleat the edges together or use a fork to mark the edges. Continue until you have used up all the filling.

Heat the oil in a large pan and fry the empanadas until golden. Sprinkle with caster sugar and serve warm.

CHOCLO (SWEETCORN FILLING)

Melt the butter in a frying pan and gently cook the spring onions. Add the green pepper, choclo and enough béchamel sauce to bind everything together, then cook over a medium heat for 3–4 minutes.

Remove the pan from the heat and add the parsley, grated cheese, a pinch of chilli or cayenne and some salt and pepper. Proceed in the same way as for meat empanadas above.

DUCK À L'ORANGE

A perfect supper for two. Traditionally, you use a whole duck, but our version is so much easier.
Use the delicious fat from the duck to make the best sautéed potatoes.

SERVES 2

2 fresh duck breasts
½ smallish onion, sliced into slim wedges
2 small garlic cloves, crushed
4 tbsp brandy
75ml red wine
finely grated zest of 1 large orange
freshly squeezed juice of 3 large oranges (about 175ml)
1 tsp cornflour
sea salt flakes
freshly ground black pepper

Preheat the oven to 180°C/Gas 4. Prick the duck skin a few times all over with a fork to allow the fat to run out while cooking. Season both sides of the duck with salt and pepper.

Heat a large non-stick frying pan over a medium heat. Add the duck breasts, skin-side down, and cook them for 5 minutes until the skin is golden brown. Turn the breasts over and cook on the other side for 3 minutes. Put the duck on a baking tray and finish cooking in the oven for a further 5 minutes.

While the duck is roasting, drain all but a tablespoon of the duck fat from the frying pan into a bowl. Return the pan to the heat and add the onion. Fry gently for 5 minutes, stirring regularly until softened and pale golden brown. Add the garlic for the last 2 minutes of the cooking time.

Remove the duck from the oven and leave to rest for 5 minutes. Pour the brandy into the pan with the softened onion and allow it to bubble for a few seconds. Add the red wine and simmer together for about a minute, stirring to lift any ducky sediment from the bottom of the pan.

Stir in the orange juice and zest, return to the boil and cook for 2–3 minutes or until the liquid has reduced by half. Mix the cornflour with 2 teaspoons of cold water in a small bowl until smooth. Stir into the orange sauce and cook for 1–2 minutes more, stirring regularly until the sauce is thickened and glossy.

Pour any juices that have collected from the resting duck into the sauce and simmer for a few seconds, while stirring. If you prefer a smooth sauce, strain it through a sieve into a jug before serving. Carve the duck into diagonal slices and serve on warmed plates with the sauce and some tasty veg.

Our timing is just right if you like your duck a little pink inside. If you prefer your meat well done, roast for 4 – 5 minutes longer.

CREAMY HADDOCK MORNAY

This recipe makes a great light meal for four people or a small starter for six. Serve just as it is for a starter or add a few new potatoes and some peas for a main course. If you like, you can add some cooked peeled prawns or scallops to the hot sauce. A few tiny lightly cooked broccoli florets or asparagus tips can also make a nice addition and because the gratins are grilled rather than baked, the vegetables should retain their colour.

SERVES 4–6

300ml whole milk
1 small onion, peeled and cut into 6 wedges
1 bay leaf
2 long strips of lemon peel
450g thick fresh haddock fillet (or other decent white fish with skin)
40g butter
25g plain flour
2 tbsp white wine or vermouth (optional)
50g Gruyère cheese, finely grated
½ tsp prepared English mustard
3 tbsp double cream
sea salt flakes
freshly ground black pepper

GRATIN TOPPING

25g fresh white breadcrumbs
15g Gruyère cheese, finely grated
½ tsp dried parsley

If you are preparing these ahead of time, cool, cover and chill before the topping is added. Instead of grilling, sprinkle the topping over the top and cook in a preheated oven at 220°C/Gas 7 for 12–15 minutes until golden brown and bubbling. ⟶

Place 4–6 small, shallow flameproof dishes on a baking tray. To make the gratin topping, mix the breadcrumbs, cheese and parsley and set aside while you make the filling.

Pour the milk into a large, deep frying pan and add the onion, bay leaf and lemon peel. Place the fish skin-side down in the pan and bring to a gentle simmer over a medium heat. Cook for 5–6 minutes, basting the fish occasionally with the milk until only just cooked. Leave to stand for 5 minutes. During the standing time the fish will continue to cook, so it is important not to simmer it for too long first.

Drain the fish in a colander over a large jug. Melt the butter in a large non-stick saucepan and stir in the flour with a wooden spoon until thoroughly combined. Slowly add the warm milk, stirring constantly over a medium heat. Bring the sauce to a simmer and continue stirring until it is smooth and thick. Stir in the wine or vermouth, if using, cheese, mustard and cream. Cook over a low heat for a further 2–3 minutes, while stirring. Season with salt and freshly ground black pepper to taste.

Flake the fish into chunky pieces and discard the skin, onion, bay leaf and lemon peel. Add the fish to the pan and heat very gently in the hot sauce for a couple of minutes to warm it through. Stir once or twice, but try not to break up the lovely chunks of fish too much.

While the fish is warming, preheat the grill to hot and place the baking tray with the shallow dishes under the heat to warm for a few seconds. Carefully remove them from the heat and divide the hot fish mixture between the warm dishes. Sprinkle with the breadcrumb mix and return to the grill for 3–5 minutes or until the tops are nicely browned.

SIMPLE CHICKEN CURRY

Helen Mills learned these recipes from her Guyanese dad, who met and married her mum in Northern Ireland, when he was in the RAF in the 1950s. Helen remembers how difficult it could be at that time to find some of the ingredients needed for her dad's favourite dishes – it's much easier now!

SERVES 4–6

1 medium chicken, jointed into 8 pieces
3 tbsp mild or hot curry powder, according to taste
2–3 tbsp vegetable oil
2 medium onions, sliced
2–3 garlic cloves, finely sliced
2 medium waxy potatoes, chopped
2 red chillies, deseeded and finely chopped
2 tbsp garam masala
600ml chicken stock
3–4 spring onions, to garnish

Rub the skin of the chicken pieces with 2 tablespoons of curry powder and leave them overnight to absorb the flavours.

Heat 2 tablespoons of oil in a pan and fry the chicken until well browned all over. Remove the chicken from the pan and set aside. Add a little more oil if needed, then fry the onions, garlic, potatoes and red chillies until the onions have softened.

Put the chicken back in the pan and sprinkle over the remaining curry powder and 2 tablespoons of garam masala, then mix well. Add enough chicken stock to barely cover the ingredients, then bring to the boil. Simmer gently until the potatoes are cooked and the chicken is tender. Sprinkle with chopped spring onions and serve with boiled rice and roti.

ROTI

MAKES 6

225g self-raising flour
½ tsp salt
1 tbsp vegetable oil, plus extra for brushing and cooking the roti

Cooked roti can be frozen and reheated in a frying pan or wrapped in foil and heated in a warm oven for a few minutes.

Put the flour and salt in a large bowl. Sprinkle over the oil and add enough water to make a soft, but not sticky, dough – add more flour if needed. Knead gently and leave to rest for about 30 minutes if you have time.

Divide the dough into 6 pieces and roll each one into a thin circle, about the thickness of a 20 pence coin. Brush the bottom third with oil and fold it towards the middle. Repeat with the top third, then turn the roti a quarter turn clockwise and repeat this process. Leave to rest again if you have time.

Heat a little oil in a heavy-based pan. Roll out a roti thinly and fry on one side until it puffs up and is speckled brown. Turn it over and repeat. Remove from the heat, allow it to cool for a few seconds and clap corner to corner to separate the layers. Fold into 4 and wrap in a tea towel placed in a colander until ready to eat. Cook the rest in the same way and serve warm.

TOFFEE APPLES

**To make really good toffee, you'll need a sugar thermometer. You'll need some
wooden lolly sticks too and you can buy these from cookware shops or even hobby shops.
If you like, use treacle instead of syrup to make treacle toffee apples. Yum, yum!**

SERVES 6

6 medium apples
350g demerara sugar
100g golden syrup
35g butter
½ tsp ground mixed spice
1 cinnamon stick

Take great care to avoid splashing yourself with any of the molten toffee. It's mind-blowingly hot and it can cause very nasty burns. Best to keep the kids well away from the stove while you're making the toffee.

To prepare the apples for coating in toffee, scrub the skins well in warm water. Pat them dry with kitchen paper and remove the stalks. Push a wooden lolly stick firmly into each apple. Line a baking tray with baking parchment.

Put the sugar, golden syrup, butter, 150ml of water, spice and cinnamon stick into a medium saucepan, over a low heat. Stir occasionally until the sugar has completely dissolved. Place a clip-on sugar thermometer in the pan. The sugar syrup will be heated to an extremely high temperature, so don't be tempted to touch or taste from the pan at any stage.

Increase the heat under the pan to medium-high and bring the sugar syrup to the boil. Continue boiling for about 10 minutes, without stirring, then carefully remove the cinnamon stick with metal tongs. Leave the toffee boiling until it reaches just over 150°C or the hard crack stage on your thermometer.

If you don't have a thermometer, have a large mug of very cold water beside the hob. Drip a little hot toffee from a long-handled spoon into the water and it should form thin, brittle threads that harden immediately.

When the toffee is ready, stir once or twice with a long-handled wooden spoon. Remove from the heat and slightly tilt the pan so that the toffee runs to one side. One by one, turn the apples around in the toffee, making sure they are evenly coated on all sides. Slowly spin the apples above the toffee for a few seconds more until the toffee is no longer dripping. Place the apples on the prepared baking tray and leave them to set. The toffee coating should become hard fairly quickly and when cooled the apples can be wrapped loosely in cellophane and tied with pretty ribbons. Eat these the day you make them.

NEPALESE COMMUNITY, OXFORDSHIRE

There is a growing community of Nepalese in Oxford, most of them ex-Gurkha soldiers and their families who have opted to settle in the area after their excellent service in the British Army. The aim of this organisation, established in 2006, is to promote, preserve and share traditional Nepalese culture, customs and values. This is one of the great recipes that the Community brought to our recipe fair.

LAMB CHHOEYLA
(NEPALESE GRILLED LAMB)

This is a classic Nepalese recipe that can also be made with chicken or pork.

SERVES 6

1.3kg boneless lamb chops
2 tbsp mustard oil

MARINADE

1 tbsp cumin powder
1 tsp turmeric
¼ tsp grated nutmeg
½ tsp timur (Szechwan pepper)
2 tbsp lemon juice
1 tbsp chilli paste
1 tbsp garlic paste
1 tbsp ginger paste
pinch of asafoetida
2 tbsp vegetable oil

CHHOEYLA SAUCE

1 tbsp cumin seeds, toasted
5 red chillies, cut into julienne strips
3 garlic cloves, halved
2.5cm piece of root ginger, sliced
pinch of asafoetida
½ tsp turmeric
1 tbsp vegetable oil

GARNISH

2 tbsp vegetable oil
1 tsp fenugreek
10 garlic cloves, thinly sliced
½ bunch of spring onions, chopped

Mix all the marinade ingredients together in a large bowl. Add the lamb chops and mix to coat them thoroughly. Set aside for 2 hours.

To make the sauce, place the cumin seeds, chillies, garlic, ginger, asafoetida and turmeric in a blender. Add the oil and a little salt and pepper, then blitz until you have a smooth paste.

Grill the meat on a barbecue until cooked through, then cut into small cubes.

In a bowl, mix the chhoeyla sauce with the meat. Slowly add the 2 tablespoons of mustard oil and toss well so that all the meat is well coated.

For the garnish, heat the oil in a non-stick pan and add the fenugreek. Fry until it turns dark, then add the garlic slices and fry until light brown. Pour this over the marinated meat, then add the spring onions and toss well. Serve with stir-fried vegetables and rice.

Posh nosh

DOUBLE CHEESE SOUFFLÉS

A punchy mixture of mature Cheddar and Gruyère makes these soufflés hard to beat. They're ideal for a dinner party as they can be prepared a day ahead and baked for 10 minutes just before serving.

SERVES 6

1 small onion, peeled and cut into wedges
275ml whole milk
1 bay leaf
40g butter, plus extra for greasing
40g plain flour
100g mature Cheddar cheese, coarsely grated
1 tsp English mustard or 2 tsp Dijon mustard
freshly grated nutmeg
3 large eggs
1 heaped tbsp chopped chives, plus extra for garnish
50g Gruyère cheese or mature Cheddar, finely grated
6 tbsp double cream
sea salt flakes
freshly ground black pepper

Butter 6 x 150ml ovenproof ramekins and line the bases with baking parchment. Place on a baking tray. Put the onion into a pan with the milk and bay leaf. Bring to a gentle simmer over a low heat and cook for 5 minutes. Watch carefully so it doesn't boil over. Take off the heat and set aside for a couple of minutes.

Preheat the oven to 200°C/Gas 6. Melt the butter in a medium non-stick saucepan over a low heat. Stir in the flour with a wooden spoon and cook for a minute or so, while stirring. Take off the heat. Strain the milk through a sieve into a jug and discard the onion and bay leaf. (You'll need around 250ml of infused milk.)

Return the butter and flour paste to the hob and gradually stir in the milk. Cook for 2 minutes, stirring constantly, until the sauce is smooth and thick. Add the Cheddar, mustard and a grating of nutmeg and cook for 1–2 minutes more until the cheese melts. Stir in the chives and season to taste. Transfer the cheese sauce to a heatproof bowl and leave to stand for 5 minutes.

Separate the eggs and, one at a time, stir the yolks into the cheese sauce until thoroughly mixed. Whisk the egg whites until stiff but not dry. Fold roughly a fifth of the egg whites into the cheese mixture with a large metal spoon, then gently fold in the rest. Spoon the soufflé mixture into the ramekins until it almost reaches the top. Bake in the centre of the oven for 20 minutes until very well risen and golden brown on top. Remove the tray from the oven and leave the soufflés to cool in the ramekins.

When the soufflés are cold, line a baking tray with baking parchment. Slide a knife around the edge of each ramekin and carefully turn the soufflés out onto your hand. Tip the right way up again and place on the tray. The soufflés can now be covered with clingfilm and chilled for up to 24 hours before baking.

Fifteen minutes before serving, preheat the oven to 200°C/Gas 6. Uncover the soufflés and sprinkle with the grated Gruyère. Spoon a tablespoon of double cream over each soufflé and allow to run down the sides. Bake for 10 minutes until hot and the cheese topping melts. Serve immediately.

LAMB CUTLETS IN PASTRY
WITH RED WINE GRAVY

A posh dinner that's much easier to make than it looks. Choose lovely British lamb, good-quality puff pastry and decent red wine and you can't go wrong.

SERVES 4

1 well-trimmed rack of lamb
or 8 lamb cutlets
1 tbsp sunflower oil
plain flour, for rolling
500g ready-made puff pastry
4 tsp mint jelly
1 egg, beaten
sea salt flakes
freshly ground black pepper

RED WINE GRAVY
150ml red wine
200ml lamb stock (made with
½ lamb stock cube)
1 tbsp redcurrant jelly
1 tsp cornflour

Put the rack of lamb on a board and cut into 8 cutlets. Season the cutlets all over with salt and pepper. Heat the oil in a large non-stick frying pan. Fry the cutlets in batches over a medium heat for 2 minutes on each side until nicely browned. Transfer to a plate and leave to cool.

To make the gravy, return the frying pan to the heat and pour in the red wine. Stir to lift the sticky sediment from the bottom of the pan. Bubble for 30 seconds or so, then add the lamb stock and redcurrant jelly. Bring to the boil and cook for 2–3 minutes or until the liquid has reduced by half.

Mix the cornflour with 2 teaspoons of cold water in a small bowl until smooth and stir into the frying pan. Stir in any juices from the lamb and cook the gravy for a minute more until thickened and glossy. Season and pour into a small pan. Set aside until you are ready to cook the cutlets.

Line a large baking tray with baking parchment. Sprinkle a light dusting of flour over your work surface and roll out the pastry until roughly 30 x 30cm square and about 3mm thick. Cut 8 squares, each measuring about 10–12cm, from the pastry – depending on the size of the cutlets.

Place half a teaspoon of mint jelly just off centre on each pastry square and put a cutlet on top, towards one of the corners. Brush the pastry edges lightly with the beaten egg and fold the remaining 3 corners of the pastry over the lamb. Wrap firmly around the meat, leaving the bone bare if possible. Turn the parcels over and place on the lined tray. The parcels can now be put in the fridge for a few hours or even overnight, if you like, until you are ready to bake them.

Preheat the oven to 200°C/Gas 6. Bake the cutlets for 20 minutes until risen and golden brown. Reheat the gravy until bubbling and simmer for a minute or two, while stirring. Check the seasoning and serve with the cutlets.

STUFFED MARROW
(ARABALI BILL MIMLI)

Avis Davies was born and brought up in Wales and has lived there all her life. But this family recipe is based on one that her children's grandmother picked up when living in Malta. Avis says that Arabali bill mimli is the family name for the dish and it was her first taste of Mediterranean ingredients, like garlic and tomato paste. She likes to serve this in summer while marrows are plentiful.

SERVES 4–6

1 medium marrow, cut in half
5 garlic cloves
3 tbsp chopped fresh thyme
3 tbsp olive oil, plus extra for brushing the marrow
2 large onions, roughly chopped
500g beef mince
2 tbsp tomato purée
2 tbsp sundried tomato paste
450g fresh tomatoes, peeled and chopped or 1 x 400g can of tomatoes
3 finely chopped tbsp fresh parsley, plus extra for serving
3 eggs, beaten
75g Parmesan cheese, grated, plus extra for serving
75g Pecorino cheese, grated
salt and black pepper

Bring a pan of lightly salted water to the boil – the pan needs to be large enough to hold the marrow. Scoop out the seeds and stringy pulp from the marrow and discard them. Then scoop out some of the flesh from the sides and reserve that for later – you need about 120g. Place the marrow in the pan of boiled water, then turn off the heat and leave it sitting in the hot water until you are ready to use it.

Crush the garlic and fresh thyme in a pestle and mortar and add salt and pepper. Chop up the reserved flesh from the marrow. Heat the olive oil in a pan, add the onions, garlic and thyme, then fry until soft. Add the mince and cook for about 10 minutes until nicely browned. Add the tomato purée and sundried tomato paste and cook for another 5 minutes. Stir in the tomatoes, chopped marrow and parsley and cook for about 10 minutes, stirring occasionally.

Take the sauce off the heat and let it cool slightly before stirring in the eggs – if the eggs are stirred in too soon they will scramble. Then add half the cheeses, stir well and cook for 5 minutes.

Line a baking tin with foil, allowing enough to wrap around the marrow. Preheat the oven to 180°C/Gas 4. Once the sauce is cooked, carefully take the 2 halves of marrow out of the hot water and place them in the baking tin. Spoon the sauce mixture into the marrow halves until they are full. Gently put the halves together and brush the skin with olive oil. Sprinkle the rest of the grated cheeses over the top of the marrow. Wrap the marrow in the foil, leaving a gap at the top.

Bake in the preheated oven for about 45 minutes, then turn the oven up to 200°/Gas 6, open out the foil and cook for another 5 minutes so the cheesy top can crisp and brown – tastes wonderful. Take the marrow out of the oven and leave it for 10 minutes. To serve, cut the marrow into rings full of juicy sauce and sprinkle with extra Parmesan cheese and parsley.

Don't worry if some of the sauce spills over the edges when you're filling the marrow. It adds a lovely flavour to the dish.

BARA BRITH & BUTTER PUDDING
WITH RUM SAUCE

Avis told us that she loves making bara brith, a recipe which was resurrected by her son Dylan and given a rum twist. It's a joy to make in the winter as everything has to be kept warm – the basins, the flour, your hands and the room – and the smell of the loaf baking in the oven is wonderful. You have to start the night before by soaking the fruit in Earl Grey tea and a splash of dark rum. Bara brith makes a great bread and butter pudding and is also delicious served sliced and buttered for tea.

SERVES 6

225g dried fruit
Earl Grey tea
splash of dark rum (optional)
450g strong white flour
75g butter, at room temperature, plus extra for greasing the tin
1 packet of dried yeast
55g sugar
1 tsp of salt
2 tsp mixed spice
1 egg, beaten
500ml milk, warmed
1 tbsp honey, warmed

EXTRAS FOR BARA BRITH AND BUTTER PUDDING
600ml full fat milk
175g double cream
120g caster sugar
6 large eggs, beaten
1 vanilla pod, split and seeds removed
butter, for spreading
100g dried or fresh fruit
lemon zest
2 tbsp demerara sugar

RUM SAUCE
55g butter
55g plain flour
350ml whole milk
120ml double cream
75g caster sugar
3 tbsp rum

The night before making the bara brith, put the dried fruit in a bowl and add enough Earl Grey tea to cover it. Add the rum and soak overnight to make the fruit plump and succulent.

Put all the ingredients out in the kitchen so that they are at room temperature when you make the bara brith. Sift the flour into a warm bowl and rub in the butter with your fingertips until the mixture resembles breadcrumbs. Add the yeast, sugar, salt and spice and mix together.

Add the beaten egg and warmed milk and knead into the dry ingredients to make a dough. The dough should look smooth and come away from the sides of the bowl to form a ball – this should take about 20 minutes. Put the bowl in a warm place, sprinkle the dough with flour and cover with a damp tea towel. Leave for about an hour and a half, by which time the mixture should have doubled in size.

Then knock back the dough – this simply means punching the dough to get all the air out of it – add the dried fruit and mix it into the dough thoroughly. Shape the dough into a loaf and place it in a large buttered loaf tin. Cover again and leave to rise for about 30 minutes. Preheat the oven to 180°C/Gas 4.

Once risen, the dough should fill the loaf tin. Bake it in the preheated oven for 20 minutes. Take it out and brush with honey while still hot. Leave to cool slightly in the tin, then turn out onto a wire rack and glaze again with warm honey.

BARA BRITH AND BUTTER PUDDING
To make the custard, pour the milk, cream and sugar into a pan and heat almost to boiling point. Take the pan off the heat and let the mixture cool before adding the beaten eggs – if the mixture is too hot when you add the eggs, it will split. Stir until the mixture thickens slightly, then add the vanilla seeds.

Slice the bara brith, butter each piece and cut into triangles. Lay the slices in an ovenproof pudding dish. Sprinkle with dried fruit or fresh fruit and a little lemon zest if you like.

Preheat the oven to 180°C/Gas 4. Pour the custard mixture over the bara brith. Sprinkle the top of the pudding with demerara sugar. Bake for about 30 minutes, then serve hot with rum sauce.

To make the rum sauce, melt the butter in a small pan. Add the flour and work it into the butter mixture with a wooden spoon to make a smooth paste. Slowly add in the milk and cream stirring constantly until you have a thick creamy sauce. Stir in the sugar and let this cook into the sauce for about 5 minutes. Take off the heat and leave to cool before adding the rum.

When you pour the custard mixture over the bara brith, don't worry if it looks like a lot – the bara brith will soak it up.

BEEF OLIVES

This is a cracking recipe and it's two for the price of one, really – a bit of steak with a meatloaf filling. Try making Scottish beef olives too, replacing some of the beef and breadcrumbs with oatmeal.

SERVES 4

2½ tbsp sunflower oil
4 rindless smoked streaky bacon rashers, chopped fairly small
1 small onion, finely chopped
4 x 150g slices of topside beef
4 tsp prepared English mustard
250g sausage meat or minced pork
25g fresh white breadcrumbs
½ tsp dried mixed herbs
finely grated zest of ½ lemon
3 tbsp plain flour
15g butter
1 medium onion, finely sliced
200ml red wine
300ml beef stock (made with 1 beef stock cube)
1 tbsp tomato purée
1 bay leaf
sea salt flakes
freshly ground black pepper

Be careful not to tie the beef olives too tightly or the filling will bulge out as they cook.

Heat 1 tablespoon of the oil in a large non-stick frying pan. Add the chopped onion and bacon to the pan and fry gently until the onion is soft, stirring regularly. Remove from the heat, transfer to a bowl and set aside to cool for 15–20 minutes.

Put one of the slices of beef on a chopping board and cover with a sheet of clingfilm. Beat with a rolling pin until roughly the thickness of a £2 coin. Cut in half widthways and spread thinly with mustard. Put to one side. Repeat with the rest of the beef and mustard. Preheat the oven to 160°C/Gas 3.

Mix the onion and bacon with the sausage meat or pork mince, breadcrumbs, herbs and lemon zest and season well. Divide the stuffing between the beef slices, spreading evenly. Roll up each piece of beef, starting at the narrow end, to make 8 beef olives. Secure the rolls by tying each end with string.

Sift the flour onto a plate and season well with salt and pepper. Roll the beef olives in the flour until lightly coated. Melt the butter with a tablespoon of the remaining oil in a non-stick frying pan over a medium heat. Fry the beef olives, 4 at a time, until browned on all sides, turning regularly. Transfer to a flameproof casserole dish as soon as they are browned.

Return the frying pan to the heat and add the rest of the oil. Gently fry the sliced onion until softened and lightly browned, stirring regularly. Tip the onion into the casserole with the beef olives. Pour the wine into the frying pan and bubble for a few seconds, stirring to deglaze any juices and sediment from the bottom. Pour into the casserole and add the beef stock, tomato purée and bay leaf. Stir gently and bring to a simmer.

Cover the casserole with a lid and cook in the centre of the oven for about 1½ hours or until the beef is tender and the sauce is thickened and glossy. Turn the beef olives in the sauce halfway through the cooking time. Serve with potatoes and green vegetables.

ASPARAGUS & LEEK BLINTZES
WITH Y FENNI CHEESE

Ruth Joseph lives in Wales. Her mother, Judith, escaped Nazi Germany at the age of 12 and nostalgically taught Ruth all her recipes, which Ruth still cooks today. Blintzes are a type of pancake and she has given them a modern Welsh twist by using Y Fenni cheese.

SERVES 8–10

FILLING
1 tbsp butter
1 tbsp olive oil
250g leeks, washed and finely chopped
250g fresh asparagus

BLINTZES
400g plain flour
pinch of salt
800ml whole milk
4 organic free-range eggs
50ml olive oil
100g butter, melted
oil, for frying

CHEESE SAUCE
50g butter
50g flour
600ml milk, warm
150g Y Fenni cheese, grated

Start by making the filling. Heat the butter and oil in a pan, add the chopped leeks and cook gently until soft, taking care that they don't brown. Trim the woody ends off the asparagus and lay them on top of the leeks. Pour in 120ml of water, put a lid on the pan and cook the asparagus with the leeks for about 3 minutes.

To make the batter for the blintzes, sift the flour into a bowl and add the salt. Whisk the milk and eggs together, then mix them into the flour. Add the olive oil and melted butter and whisk well. Alternatively, you can put all the batter ingredients, except the oil for frying, in a food processor and mix. Pour the batter into a jug and leave to stand in the fridge.

To make the cheese sauce, melt the butter in a pan and stir in the flour. Slowly add the warm milk and cook for 10 minutes. Stir in the grated cheese and set aside.

Put a non-stick frying pan over a medium-high heat and brush the pan with oil. Pour a little batter into the pan and swirl around until the base of the pan is covered. Cook for 1–2 minutes, then flip over and cook for about a minute more. Put the pancake on a plate and continue until all the mixture is used up. Put sheets of baking parchment between each pancake so that they don't stick together. Preheat the oven to 180°C/Gas 4.

Now stuff the blintzes. Take one, add a spoonful of filling and a good tablespoon of cheese sauce, then roll it up neatly and place in an ovenproof dish. Continue until all the pancakes and filling are used up, then pour over the rest of the cheese sauce. Bake for 20 minutes until piping hot and golden on top.

ORCHID GATEAU

Ruth explained to us that she evolved this recipe for a yeast-based cake when she baked for the Orchid Room, a select restaurant that was at the top of a department store in Cardiff. When she bakes, Ruth is proud to use her mother's cake tin which she brought with her from Germany.

SERVES 10–12

DOUGH
300ml fresh milk,
1 vanilla pod, split and seeds scraped out
400g strong plain flour, plus extra for sprinkling
3 tsp dried yeast
3 tbsp soft brown sugar
4 large organic eggs, beaten
pinch of salt
grated zest of 1 lemon
grated zest of ½ orange
200g butter, softened, plus extra for greasing
natural pink colouring (optional)

SUGAR SYRUP
400g golden caster sugar
strained juice of 1 orange
good glug of Framboise

DECORATION
home-made strawberry jam or apricot jam with water for glazing
400g fresh strawberries
juice of ½ lemon
4 tbsp icing sugar
500ml whipping cream
fresh rose petals

Warm the milk gently with the vanilla seeds, just to body temperature. Pour it into a bowl and add 6 tablespoons of the flour, the yeast and the sugar. Leave in a warm place until the mixture is bubbling, then add the beaten eggs and the grated lemon and orange zest.

Put the remaining flour in a large mixing bowl with the salt, then pour in the milk and egg mixture. Add the softened butter and a drop of pink colouring and beat well until you have a sticky batter. Leave in a warm place to double in size.

Meanwhile, make the sugar syrup. Heat the sugar with the orange juice and 180ml water. Stir until the sugar is dissolved and add Framboise to taste.

Grease a 23cm cake tin and sprinkle with flour. Preheat the oven to 200°C/Gas 6. Check the cake batter and beat it for another minute, then pour it into the prepared cake tin and cover with a cloth. Leave until it has risen three-quarters of the way up the tin.

Place in the preheated oven and bake for 25–30 minutes until the cake is golden and luscious. Take the tin out of the oven and pour over the syrup, then leave to cool in the tin.

Once the cake is cold, cross your fingers and turn it out onto a plate. Warm a couple of spoonfuls of jam with a spoonful of water and brush this over the top of the cake to glaze. Mix the strawberries with the lemon juice and icing sugar and add them to the middle of the cake. Whip the cream and pipe it on top of the strawberries, then decorate the cake with more strawberries and cream. Sprinkle rose petals over and around the cake. Serve and enjoy!

ROAST LEG OF LAMB
WITH GARLIC, ANCHOVY & ROSEMARY

Britain has the best lamb in the world. There are more breeds than you can shake a crook at and all are great to eat. We always say that a roast leg of lamb makes every Sunday an event.

SERVES 4–6

1 x 2kg leg of lamb
2 fresh rosemary stalks
6–7 canned anchovy fillets in oil, drained (optional)
2 garlic cloves
1 medium onion, sliced
200ml red wine
1 tbsp redcurrant jelly
1 tbsp cornflour
½ lamb stock cube (optional)
sea salt flakes
freshly ground black pepper

If you prefer your lamb well done, cook for an extra 20 minutes and if you like your lamb fairly pink, cook for 20 minutes less.

For slow-roast lamb, wrap the leg in foil and cook at 160°C/Gas 3 for 4–5 hours, until the meat is falling of the bone. Turn the oven up to 200°C/Gas 6, remove the foil and cook the lamb for another 10 minutes to crisp the skin.

Preheat the oven to 190°C/Gas 5. Put the lamb on a board and use the tip of a knife to make 15–20 deep holes all over it. Take sprigs of rosemary off the stalks and cut each anchovy fillet, if using, into 3 pieces. Peel the garlic and cut into slivers. Between your thumb and forefinger, pinch a sprig of rosemary, a sliver of garlic and a piece of anchovy, then push this into one of the holes as far as it will go. Fill all the holes like this.

Put the sliced onion in a roasting tin and place the lamb on top, tucking the onion under the lamb as much as possible. (The onion will add colour and flavour to your gravy.) Season the lamb with salt and pepper. Roast for 1 hour and 15 minutes until the lamb is nicely browned.

Take the lamb out of the oven and, using an oven glove, tilt the pan and spoon off any fat that may have collected beneath it. Try to retain the dark cooking juices that will have seeped out of the lamb as these will be used to make the gravy. Pour the wine into the tin and cover with foil, pinching the foil around the edges of the tin to fully enclose the lamb. Return to the oven for a further 45 minutes for medium lamb. Uncover the lamb and put it on a warmed dish. Cover with the foil and a couple of tea towels and leave to rest for 15–20 minutes.

Spoon off any fat from the roasting tin, then put it on the hob and stir in 200ml water and redcurrant jelly. Bring to the boil, stirring constantly until the jelly melts and any flavoursome sediment is lifted from the bottom of the tin. Remove from the heat and pour though a sieve into a pan. Return the strained gravy to the hob and bring to a simmer. Discard the onion.

Mix the cornflour with 2 tablespoons of cold water in a bowl until smooth. Stir into the gravy, add the crumbled stock cube if using, and simmer for 2 minutes more until the gravy is thick and glossy. Season and keep on a low heat until the lamb has finished resting. Pour any juices that may have collected under the meat into the gravy and simmer for a minute or so more. Carve the lamb into slices and serve with the hot gravy.

BAKED WELSH CAKE CHEESECAKE

Derith Rhisiart likes to cook traditional Welsh dishes that she learned from her grandma, but she puts her own subtle twists on them. Here she makes Welsh cakes with cranberries and white chocolate instead of trad dried fruit and then makes them into an amazing cheesecake.

SERVES 8

WELSH CAKES
450g self-raising flour, plus extra for dusting
pinch of salt
120g lard
120g butter
120g caster sugar, plus extra for sprinkling on cooked cakes
50g white chocolate drops
75g dried cranberries, chopped
2 eggs, beaten
drop of milk, if needed

CHEESECAKE
12–14 digestive biscuits or 15 small shortbreads
50g Welsh butter
½ tsp cinnamon
½ tsp nutmeg
600g cream cheese
2 tbsp plain flour
175g caster sugar
3 drops of vanilla essence
2 eggs, plus 1 yolk
142ml soured cream
12 Welsh cakes, already cooked

Tip the flour into a large bowl and add the pinch of salt. Rub the lard and the butter together with the flour until the mixture resembles breadcrumbs. Stir in the caster sugar, then add the white chocolate and cranberries and mix well.

Add the eggs and mix with your hands until everything comes together – add a dash of milk if needed. Put the mixture on a floured surface and roll it out to a thickness of about 60mm. Cut out circles with a 5cm pastry cutter – this mixture should make about 50.

Grease a heavy frying pan or ideally a bakestone (no need to grease) and heat for 5–10 minutes on the hob. Reduce the heat and place the Welsh cakes into the hot pan and cook for about a minute or until golden brown. Turn over and cook for another minute, again until golden brown. Keep an eye on the heat to ensure that the temperature is not too hot or too cold. If too cold they will spread, if too hot, they will burn and cook on the outside too quickly. Keep repeating the process until they are firm. They will rise considerably. Place the cakes on sugared greaseproof paper and sprinkle with caster sugar.

CHEESECAKE
Preheat the oven to 180°C/Gas 4. Put the biscuits in a freezer bag and crush them with a rolling pin. Melt the butter in pan and mix in the crushed biscuits and spices. Press this mixture into a 23cm springform tin and bake for 5–10 minutes, then set aside to cool.

Whisk the cream cheese with the flour, sugar, vanilla essence, eggs and soured cream. Cut up 4 or 5 Welsh cakes into chunky bits and gently fold them into the mixture. Arrange enough of the rest of the Welsh cakes on the biscuit base until it is covered and then pour the cream mixture on top. Bake for 40 minutes – it should still be slightly wobbly in the centre. Leave to cool for a while in the tin and serve warm or cold.

FILLET STEAKS
STUFFED WITH GOAT'S CHEESE
WITH CANDIED SHALLOTS

We love this dish. The sticky, sweet shallots go really well with the cheesy surprise at the centre of the steak and the bacon keeps the steaks nice and juicy.

SERVES 4

4 good, thick, centre-cut fillet steaks
150g soft goat's cheese
1 tsp finely chopped rosemary
zest of 1 lemon
1 garlic clove, crushed
4 rindless streaky bacon rashers
2 tbsp olive oil
sea salt flakes
cracked black pepper

CANDIED SHALLOTS
12 shallots
4 tbsp butter
1 tbsp caster sugar
75ml red wine
50ml port
50ml cassis
250ml good beef stock
1 bay leaf
½ tsp dried thyme
zest of half a lemon

Take the steaks out of the fridge an hour or so before cooking so that they are at room temperature. Crumble the cheese into a bowl, then add the rosemary, lemon zest and garlic.

Cut a pocket into each steak, taking care not to cut all the way through. Place a quarter of the cheese stuffing into each pocket. Close the flap, and wrap a rasher of bacon around the side of each steak. Secure with a cocktail stick.

Rub olive oil over the steaks, then sprinkle with salt and pepper. Cook in a hot frying pan until the steak is how you like it. Brown the bacon on the edges just before you remove the steaks from the pan. Allow them to rest for 5 minutes before serving with the candied shallots.

CANDIED SHALLOTS
Bring a pan of water to the boil. Simmer the shallots in the water for 5 minutes, then drain.

Heat the butter in a frying pan, add the shallots and cook until brown. Add the sugar and stir until the butter starts to caramelise.

Mix the wine, port, cassis and stock in a jug. Add about a quarter of this to the pan of shallots, bring to the boil, then add the bay leaf, thyme and lemon zest. Keep adding the remaining liquid until the shallots are just covered with a lovely sticky glaze, then set aside until needed.

SLOW FOOD

Slow Food is an international movement, whose members believe in linking the pleasures of good food with a commitment to the environment. The aim is to encourage people to enjoy local, traditional foods that are produced to environmentally friendly standards – and that taste great. The recipe below is a good example and if you can pick the walnuts and fruit yourself – even better.

PIGEON WITH WALNUTS

This recipe can be varied to suit the season and what you have available. Use hazelnuts or Kent cobs instead of walnuts, or seasonal fruit, such as quince, apples or apricots. Soak these in the wine in the same way as the walnuts. Pigeon is best served pink so be careful not to overcook it.

SERVES 4

small handful of walnuts
sweet wine
4 pigeons
2 tbsp olive oil
sprig of fresh thyme
sea salt flakes
black pepper

The night before you want to cook this dish, put the walnuts in a bowl with sweet wine to cover. Leave to soak overnight.

To prepare the pigeons, place one on a chopping board with the breast uppermost and the head pointing away from you. Feel for the backbone and snip the skin with a pair of scissors. Peel off the skin, taking care to keep the feathers underneath. With a sharp knife, remove the breasts from the ribs, trying not to leave any meat behind. Wash the meat under a cool running tap and place on kitchen paper. The rest of the carcass should be skinned and used to make stock – throw the head and feet away. Prepare the rest of the pigeons in the same way.

Heat the olive oil in a large frying pan and add the thyme. Add the pigeon breasts and cook briefly to seal. Take the breasts out of the pan and cut into slices, taking care not to lose any of the cooking juices. Pour the walnuts and sweet wine into the frying pan, bring to boil and continue to cook until slightly reduced. Season, then add the slices of pigeon and any juices. Turn off the heat but leave on the pan on the stove. Cover the pan with a lid or some foil and leave to rest for 10 minutes.

Serve as a first course with bread for the juices or a main course with game chips.

Family
classics

DEEP-FILLED CHICKEN & MUSHROOM PIE

This classic pie has a shortcrust pastry base, creamy chicken and mushroom filling and a light puff pastry crust. It's surprisingly easy to make and will go down a treat with all the family. You'll need a pie dish that will hold around 1.2 litres.

SERVES 6

50g butter
1 small onion, finely chopped
1 garlic clove, finely chopped
250g button mushrooms (ideally chestnut mushrooms), wiped and halved
6 boneless, skinless chicken thighs
1 bay leaf
2 tsp freshly chopped thyme leaves or
½ tsp dried thyme or mixed dried herbs
1 chicken stock cube
200ml just-boiled water
50g plain flour
200ml whole milk
4–5 tbsp double or single cream
(or milk if you don't have any cream handy)
2–3 tbsp white wine (optional)
sea salt flakes
freshly ground black pepper

SHORTCRUST PASTRY

200g plain flour, plus extra for rolling
good pinch of sea salt
125g cold butter, cut into cubes
1 large egg
1 tbsp whole or semi-skimmed milk

PUFF PASTRY

500g ready-made puff pastry
(thawed if frozen)

To make the filling, melt the butter in a large non-stick frying pan over a medium-high heat. Add the onion, garlic and mushrooms and fry for 4–6 minutes, stirring often until the onion and mushrooms are lightly browned. Cut the chicken into small bite-sized pieces, season with pepper and add them to the pan with the bay leaf and thyme leaves. Cook everything for 4–5 minutes until the meat is no longer pink, turning often. Dissolve the stock cube in the 200ml of just-boiled water.

Stir the flour into the chicken mixture and cook for a few seconds before slowly adding the milk. Gradually stir in the stock and bring to a gentle simmer. Cook for 2 minutes until the sauce is smooth and thick. Season to taste, remove from the heat and stir in the cream and wine, if using. Cover the pan with clingfilm to prevent a skin from forming and set aside to cool. Preheat the oven to 190°C/Gas 5.

To make the shortcrust pastry, put the flour in a food processor and add the salt. Drop the cubes of butter on top, then blitz on the pulse setting until the mixture resembles fine breadcrumbs. Whisk the egg with the milk and pour onto the flour and butter mixture with the motor running, reserving 2 tablespoons of the egg mixture for glazing the pastry. Continue blending until the dough begins to come together. Turn out onto a lightly floured board and knead quickly into a ball. Roll out to about 4mm thick and large enough to line your pie dish. Carefully lift the pastry over your pie dish, leaving any excess pastry overhanging the edge. Spoon the cooled chicken filling into the dish and brush the pastry edge with a little of the reserved beaten egg.

Place the puff pastry on a well-floured surface and roll out until it is about 4mm thick and large enough to cover the pie. Place the puff pastry over the pie and press the edges firmly together to seal and trim neatly. Brush the top of the pastry with the beaten egg. Decorate with any pastry trimmings and brush with more beaten egg to glaze. Bake for 40–45 minutes until the crust is puffed up and golden brown and the filling is piping hot.

SAMBHAR (LENTIL SOUP)
WITH VADA (SPICY DOUGHNUTS)

Padmaja is from Andhra Pradesh in southern India and has lived in the UK for 12 years. Before coming here, she says she couldn't cook at all, but being so far from home made her want to make her family recipes. Now she has a food blog and teaches her friends how to cook her recipes!

SERVES 6

SAMBHAR
200g toor dal (yellow lentils)
1 onion, chopped
1 green chilli, chopped
2 tomatoes, chopped
1 tsp chilli powder
¼ tsp turmeric
salt to taste

TEMPERING MIXTURE
1 tbsp sunflower oil
1 tsp black mustard seeds
1 tsp cumin seeds
2 fresh curry leaves
1 tbsp sambhar powder
4–5 tbsp tamarind juice
fresh coriander

VADA
200g black gram lentils
1 tbsp rice
1 onion, finely chopped
1 green chilli, finely chopped
pinch of sodium bicarbonate
450ml sunflower oil, for deep-frying
salt to taste

First make the soup. Rinse the dal and put it in a large pan with the onion, chilli, tomatoes and spices. Add 200ml water, bring to the boil and cook for about 30 minutes until the dal is soft. Add salt to taste and set aside.

To temper the lentils, heat the sunflower oil in a large pan and add the mustard seeds and cumin seeds. When they start spluttering, add the curry leaves and sambhar powder. Fry for a minute and then add the cooked dal mixture and the tamarind juice. Check the seasoning and boil for 5 minutes. Garnish with coriander leaves and serve with the spicy doughnuts.

VADA
Soak the lentils and rice in water for 1 hour, then drain. Put them into a food processor or blender with a tablespoon or so of water and blitz to a thick batter. Add the chopped onion and the chilli, bicarbonate and salt and mix well. Set aside.

Heat the sunflower oil in a deep-fat fryer to about 180°C. To shape the doughnuts, drop about 2 tablespoons of batter onto a piece of plastic that you have moistened with water. Press it down slightly, make a hole in the middle, then carefully drop it into the hot oil. Make and fry the doughnuts a few at a time until all the mixture is used up.

SPICY SOUTH INDIAN CHICKEN CURRY

This is one of Padmaja's dad's recipes. At home, he would cook the meat dishes and her mum would make the veggie ones. We loved this curry and we thought Padmaja's food was some of the most enjoyable we had when filming the 'Mums Know Best' series.

SERVES 4

2.5cm piece of fresh root ginger
3 garlic cloves
1 tbsp sunflower oil
1 onion, finely sliced
1 green chilli, sliced
2 chicken breasts, cut into small pieces
1 tsp chilli powder
¼ tsp turmeric
fresh coriander
salt to taste

MASALA PASTE
2.5cm piece of cinnamon stick
2 cardamom pods
2 cloves
1 tbsp white poppy seeds
2 tbsp coriander seeds
2 tbsp fresh coconut flesh

First make the masala paste. Grind all the ingredients together in a pestle and mortar until you have a fine paste.

Make a ginger and garlic paste by pounding the fresh ginger and garlic cloves in a pestle and mortar or by blitzing them in a small blender.

Heat the sunflower oil in a pan and fry the onion and chilli until softened. Add the masala paste and a tablespoon of the ginger and garlic paste and fry for 2–3 minutes. Now add the chicken pieces, chilli powder, turmeric and salt, cover the pan and cook for 5 minutes. Then add about 120ml of water and cook until the chicken is tender. Garnish with coriander leaves and serve with rice.

CHICKEN IN CREAMY TARRAGON SAUCE

You'll need a lidded frying pan or a wide flameproof casserole dish for making this, as the chicken breasts need to be fried until golden and then gently poached to make them extra succulent. Buy the best chicken you can afford for this dish.

SERVES 4

4 boneless chicken breasts, skin on
25g butter
1 tsp sunflower oil
1 small onion, finely chopped
1 garlic clove, finely chopped
100ml white wine
200ml chicken stock (fresh or made with
½ chicken stock cube)
small bunch (about 15g) of fresh tarragon,
plus extra sprigs for garnish
150ml double cream
sea salt flakes
freshly ground black pepper

Season the chicken breasts with a little sea salt and plenty of freshly ground black pepper. Melt the butter with the oil in a large pan and fry the chicken, skin-side down, for 3 minutes over a medium-high heat until golden.

Turn the chicken over, reduce the heat and add the onion and garlic to the pan. Cook for 2–3 minutes, stirring regularly until the onion is softened and beginning to colour.

Pour the wine into the pan and let it bubble furiously for 30 seconds, then stir in the stock and 2 of the tarragon sprigs. Cover the pan with a lid and leave to simmer very gently for 10–12 minutes or until the chicken is just cooked.

Transfer the chicken to a warmed plate to rest and remove the tarragon sprigs from the pan. Turn up the heat and bring the cooking liquor to the boil. Cook for about 5 minutes or until the liquid has reduced by half. Strip the leaves from the remaining tarragon sprigs and chop them fairly small.

Stir the cream and tarragon into the pan and simmer for 2–3 minutes longer, stirring occasionally until the sauce is thick enough to coat the back of a spoon. Return the chicken breasts to the pan and heat through for a minute or so. Serve with green beans and new potatoes, garnished with small sprigs of tarragon if you like.

THE JONES BOYS' FAVOURITE CHICKEN & MUSHROOM CRUMBLE

Victoria Jones learned many of her recipes from her grandma and inherited her
treasured cookery books and some of her kitchen equipment. This is a family favourite
and a good filling meal, ideal for feeding Victoria's three hungry sons and their friends.

SERVES 6

4 chicken breasts, boned and skinned
4 chicken thighs, boned and skinned
1 tbsp olive oil
1 large onion, finely chopped
2 garlic cloves, crushed
250g chestnut mushrooms, sliced
5 smoked back bacon rashers, chopped
1 x 295g can of condensed
mushroom soup
150ml double or single cream
150ml chicken stock
freshly ground black pepper

CRUMBLE TOPPING
100g cold butter
200g plain flour
50g mature Cheddar cheese, grated
50g porridge oats

Cut the chicken breasts and thighs into bite-sized pieces.
Heat the oil in a large pan, then add the onion and cook
gently over a low heat until soft and lightly coloured – this
should take about 8 minutes. Add the crushed garlic and
cook for another 2 minutes.

Turn up the heat, then add the mushrooms and bacon and
fry until both are cooked through. Add the chicken, followed
by the soup, cream and stock. Season with black pepper – the
bacon should add enough salt. Stir, put a lid on the pan and
simmer for 10–15 minutes or until the chicken is cooked.

Meanwhile, put all the ingredients for the crumble mixture in
a food processor and pulse until well mixed. Alternatively, rub
the butter into the flour with your fingertips until the mixture
resembles breadcrumbs and then stir in the cheese and
porridge oats.

Preheat the oven to 190°C/Gas 5. Once the chicken and
mushroom mixture is cooked, tip it into an ovenproof dish
and spread the crumble mixture over the top. Cook in the
preheated oven for about 15 minutes until the crumble is
crispy on top and the chicken sauce is bubbling up from
underneath.

This recipe can be prepared up to 24 hours ahead and left
in the fridge. It should then be cooked for about 30 minutes
until the crumble is crispy on top and the sauce is bubbling.

You can also freeze the prepared crumble. Defrost thoroughly
and cook in the preheated oven for about 30 minutes as before.
Serve with potatoes and green vegetables or salad.

MUM'S EVERYDAY FISH PIE
WITH CHEESY MASH

We've given you the ultimate fish pie, now here's the everyday version, without all the palava – a good, quick family feast.

SERVES 4–5

400ml whole milk
1 small onion, thickly sliced
2 bay leaves
500g skinned thick white fish fillets, such as cod, haddock or pollock
40g butter
40g plain flour
150g frozen peas
200g large North Atlantic prawns, thawed if necessary and peeled
sea salt flakes
freshly ground black pepper

TOPPING

800g medium potatoes, peeled and cut into even-sized pieces
40g butter, cubed
3 tbsp milk
100g mature Cheddar cheese, grated

To make the filling, pour the milk into a large pan and add the sliced onion and bay leaves. Season with salt and pepper. Place the fish fillets in the pan and bring to a very gentle simmer, then cover and cook for 2 minutes. Remove from the heat and leave to stand and infuse for 20 minutes. Drain the fish through a colander into a bowl, then pour the milk into a jug.

Meanwhile, make the mash. Half fill a large saucepan with cold water. Add the potatoes and bring to the boil, then reduce the heat and simmer for 15 minutes or until the potatoes are soft. Drain the potatoes and return them to the pan, then mash with the butter, milk and three-quarters of the grated cheese. Season to taste. Preheat the oven to 200°C/Gas 6.

Now, finish the filling. Melt the butter in a medium saucepan and stir in the flour. Cook for a few seconds, then gradually add the infused milk, stirring over a medium heat for 3–4 minutes until the sauce is smooth and thick. Stir in the peas and season with salt and black pepper.

Spread a third of the sauce into the base of a 1.5 litre ovenproof dish. Scatter half the fish fillets over the sauce, breaking them into chunky pieces as you go and discarding the onion and bay leaves. Drop half the prawns on top and pour over another third of the sauce. Continue with the layers and finish with the final third of sauce.

Spoon the potato over the fish mixture, then fork the surface and sprinkle with the remaining cheese. Place the dish on a baking tray and bake in the centre of the oven for about 25 minutes or until the top is golden and the filling is bubbling.

It's important to layer the fish pie up like this so the fish remains in good chunky pieces.

BASIC PASTA SAUCE

Rosita Minichiello's parents are Italian and Rosita learned her cooking skills from her mum. As a child, she believed her mother had special flavour in her hands and that was why her food tasted good!

MAKES ENOUGH FOR 1.5KG OF PASTA

5 tbsp olive oil
1 medium white onion, peeled
1 celery stick, washed
1 carrot, scrubbed
1 clove of garlic, peeled
500g beef bones (optional)
3 rounded dsrtsp tomato purée
4 x 400g cans of plum tomatoes in rich tomato sauce
1 x 680g jar of tomato passata
2 tsp sea salt flakes
1 bouquet garni (optional)
2 bay leaves (optional)
50ml Marsala wine
splash of balsamic vinegar
15–20 basil leaves, washed and torn
salt and pepper

Heat the oil in a large heavy pan and add the whole onion, celery stick, carrot and garlic clove, with the beef bones, if using. Allow everything to brown. When the bones and vegetables have taken on a good colour, add the tomato purée, canned tomatoes and passata. Fill the tomato cans with water and add that to the pan too. Add salt and the herbs, if using.

Bring to the boil and cover the pan with a heavy lid. Reduce the heat so that the sauce just turns over at a simmer. Leave to cook for at least 2 hours but ideally for 4–5 hours. When the fat on the top of the sauce looks dark, you know it is ready. Stir the sauce occasionally while it cooks and as it reduces, top it up from a kettle of boiling water and allow it to reduce again.

After the final reduction, remove the bones, vegetables, bouquet garni and bay leaves. Add the Marsala, balsamic vinegar and basil leaves. Check the seasoning and add salt and pepper if needed, then the sauce is ready.

EVERYDAY MINESTRA

This is an everyday minestra (veg dish) made by Gerarda, Rosita's mum. She used cabbage, spinach, spring greens, kale – whatever was available – but a favourite was endive, which she called scarole.

SERVES 4

1 large bag of fresh greens
glug of extra virgin olive oil
splash of balsamic vinegar
2 garlic cloves, thinly sliced
salt and pepper

Wash the greens in a couple of changes of water and put them into a large pan with some boiling, salted water. Stir the leaves to get them wilting in the hot water. Cook for a few minutes until ready – endive or spinach will only need a minute or two but cabbage will take longer. Refresh the leaves in cold water to stop them cooking.

In a serving bowl, mix a good glug of good olive oil with a splash of balsamic and the garlic, then season to taste. Drain the greens and then squeeze in handfuls until most of the water is gone. Cut or tear the leaves into smaller pieces. Add the greens to the dressing and mix well, lifting the leaves with a couple of forks. Serve while still just warm.

GERARDA MINICHIELLO'S MEATBALLS

Rosita's mum has never officially given her this recipe. She's had to work it out for herself!

MAKES ABOUT 30

100g sourdough bread
(preferably with no added yeast)
6 sprigs of thyme
12 sage leaves
24 mint leaves
24 flat-leaf parsley leaves
5 garlic cloves, finely chopped
100g pine nuts, toasted in a heavy pan
150g raisins
3 large eggs
Worcestershire sauce (optional)
100g Pecorino cheese, grated
500g minced lamb
500g minced beef
sunflower oil or vegetable oil, for frying
salt and pepper

Soak the sourdough bread in warm water for 2–3 minutes. Remove it and squeeze out as much water as you can, then set aside. Chop all the herbs together and mix with the garlic and toasted pine nuts. Soak the raisins in warm water for 5–10 minutes to plump them up, then drain.

Beat the eggs in a large mixing bowl and add salt and pepper and a good splash of Worcestershire sauce, if using. Add the garlic, herbs, pine nuts and grated cheese and mix well.

Break the soaked bread into small pieces and add this with the raisins to the egg mix. With very clean hands, mix in the meats and work until smooth. Use a dessertspoon to shape the mixture into balls and set these on a plate ready for frying.

Pour the oil into a heavy frying pan to a depth of about 0.5cm. Fry the meatballs, about 10 at a time, until brown, turning them several times to make sure they are browned all over.

As each batch is cooked, add them to the simmering tomato sauce (see opposite), from which the bones and veg have been removed. Once the final batch of meatballs have been added, cook them all in the sauce for another 35 minutes. Remove the meatballs to a warm dish. Serve the sauce poured onto the pasta and the meatballs on the side.

SCAPECE

This is another vegetable dish from Rosita. This was something she says she and her siblings would fight over as children. It was special as it could only be made with the very first, young, courgettes.

SERVES 4

sunflower oil, for frying
6 small to medium courgettes
2 garlic cloves, finely sliced
8 fresh mint leaves (from the garden or double if using supermarket mint), torn
6 tbsp red wine vinegar
sea salt and freshly ground black pepper

Pour the oil into a heavy frying pan to a depth of about 1cm. Cut the courgettes into slices 2–4mm thick and arrange them in a single layer. Cook until they brown, then turn them over to brown the other side. Remove and drain on kitchen paper.

Mix the remaining ingredients in a bowl, then add the cooked courgettes. Stir carefully, then cover with clingfilm. Leave for at least 4 hours or overnight if you can. Serve on good chewy bread drizzled with some olive oil and an extra grinding of salt.

ITALIAN PEAR & CHOCOLATE CAKE

Rosita has a pear tree in her garden and used some of her crop to make us
this amazing cake, traditionally served at Italian birthday parties.

SERVES 8

6 large eggs
2 tsp vanilla extract
(depending on the quality – some
are much stronger than others)
200g caster sugar
200g plain flour (preferably '00')
1 tsp baking powder
pinch of salt
cocoa powder, to serve
icing sugar, to serve

LEMON & CHOCOLATE SAUCES
grated zest and juice of 1 lemon
1 litre milk
125g flour
300g caster sugar
2 tsp vanilla extract
2 large eggs
150g dark chocolate, broken into pieces

POACHED PEARS
3 pears
slice of lemon
200g sugar
3–4 dsrtsp Amaretto
3–4 dsrtsp fresh lemon juice

Preheat the oven to 180°C/Gas 4. Grease and line a 25–30cm
cake tin. Put the eggs, vanilla and sugar in a bowl and place
over a pan of simmering water. Whisk until the mixture is
really thick – almost like a mousse. Remove from the heat.

Mix the flour with the baking powder and salt and sift into the
egg mixture. Using a slotted spoon, fold the flour into the egg.
Pour the mixture into the prepared tin and level the surface. Bake
in the lower part of the preheated oven for 15–20 minutes. It
should not wobble when done. Cool in the tin for 10 minutes, then
carefully transfer to a wire rack to cool completely.

LEMON AND CHOCOLATE SAUCES
Put the grated lemon zest and juice in a pan with 50ml of water.
Bring to the boil and reduce to a few spoonfuls, then pour into
a bowl and set aside.

Heat the milk until it is at the point of boiling. In a separate bowl,
mix the flour, sugar and vanilla with the eggs until creamy. Pour
the hot milk onto the egg mix and whisk. Quickly wash the
milk pan, then pour the milk and egg mixture into the clean
pan and bring to the boil while whisking constantly. Allow to
cook for a minute or two.

Pour half the sauce onto the lemon reduction and mix well. Add
the chocolate to the remaining sauce and mix until the chocolate
is melted by the warmth of the sauce and amalgamated. It is
best to stand the pans of sauce in a sink of cold water to cool –
that way they won't form a skin.

POACHED PEARS
Peel the pears, cut them in half lengthways and remove the seeds
and cores. Pour 500ml of water into a pan and add a slice of
lemon and the sugar. Bring to the boil. Add the pears and cook
gently for about 20 minutes or until slightly translucent – some
pears may take longer than this. Remove the pears and leave
them to cool. Slice thinly.

Conference or other firm-fleshed pears that cook well are best for this cake.

Remove the lemon slice from the sugar stock and discard. Then divide the stock between two cups. Mix the Amaretto into one cup and the lemon juice into the other.

ASSEMBLING THE CAKE

Cut the cake into 3 layers. Place the bottom layer onto a serving plate. Spoon on enough of the Amaretto stock to moisten the cake but don't let it get soggy. Carefully spread the cooled chocolate sauce on top – you may not need all of it – then add the sliced pears. Cover with another layer of cake, soak with the lemon stock and add the lemon sauce (again, you may not need all of it).

Add the final layer of cake and soak with some more of whichever stock you prefer and some of the remaining sauce. If you finish with the lemon sauce, sift a little cocoa powder on top. If you finish with the chocolate sauce, sift a little icing sugar on top. Pop the cake into the fridge for about 2 hours and then it will be ready to serve.

JAM ROLY POLY PUDDING

A much-mutilated version of this often appears in school dinners. Just have a go at making your own and you'll realise it's a great classic pud. In Si's house, jam roly poly is known as jam splat.

SERVES 6

softened butter, for greasing
200g self-raising flour, plus extra
for dusting
100g shredded suet
1 tbsp caster sugar
good pinch of fine sea salt
150ml semi-skimmed milk or water
6–7 tbsp raspberry or strawberry jam

If you're feeding vegetarians, make this with vegetable suet.

Preheat the oven to 200°C/Gas 6. Butter a sheet of baking parchment, about 38 x 38cm in size, and set aside. Bring a kettle of water to the boil and set a low rack in a smallish roasting tin.

Put the flour, suet, sugar and salt in a large bowl and mix well. Slowly add the milk or water, stirring constantly with a wooden spoon until the mixture forms a soft, spongy dough. Gather the dough and knead it lightly on a floured surface. Roll the dough out into a rectangle roughly 22 x 32cm.

Drop the jam in large spoonfuls onto the dough, leaving a 1.5cm border all the way round the outside. Gently roll up the dough from one of the short ends and carefully transfer it to the baking parchment, seam-side down. Wrap the roly poly in the parchment, making a long pleat in the parchment to allow the pudding to expand as it cooks.

Twist the ends of the parchment like a Christmas cracker to seal the pudding inside and tie tightly with kitchen string. Do the same with a large sheet of foil, making a pleat and twisting the ends to seal. Place the wrapped pudding on the rack in the roasting tin and pour just-boiled water around it. The water should not rise more than a centimetre up the sides of the pudding. Carry the tin very carefully to the oven and bake for 35 minutes.

Remove the tin and carefully lift the pudding off the rack. Unwrap the foil, then snip the string and unwrap the paper. The pudding should be well risen and lightly browned in places. Don't worry if the jam has made its way through to the outside of the pudding a little – it will taste all the more delicious. Put on a board or serving plate and cut into thick slices. Serve with lots of hot custard (see page 211) or cream.

EVE'S PUDDING

**Adam wouldn't stand a chance if tempted by Eve with this apple delight –
nor would any hungry Hairy Biker. Bring it on!**

SERVES 6

3 medium cooking apples
(roughly 600g unpeeled weight),
peeled, cored and roughly chopped
65g golden caster sugar
½ tsp ground cinnamon
juice and finely grated zest of
1 unwaxed lemon

SPONGE TOPPING
115g softened butter,
plus extra for greasing
115g golden caster sugar, plus 1 tbsp
2 large eggs, lightly beaten
½ tsp vanilla extract
125g self-raising flour
3 tbsp flaked almonds (optional)

VANILLA CUSTARD
2 large free-range egg yolks
2 heaped tsp cornflour
25g caster sugar
1 vanilla pot, split, or
½ tsp vanilla extract
250ml whole milk
250ml double cream

Preheat the oven to 180°C/Gas 4. Butter a 1.2 litre pie dish. Put the apples, sugar, cinnamon, lemon juice and zest in the pie dish and toss everything together well.

To make the topping, put the butter in a bowl with the 115g sugar. Using an electric whisk, cream the butter and sugar until light and fluffy. Gradually add half the beaten eggs, whisking well between each addition. Add the vanilla extract, then half the flour and beat well. Whisk in the rest of the eggs and fold in the remaining flour until smooth.

Spoon the cake batter on top of the apples and spread to the sides of the dish. Sprinkle with the remaining tablespoon of caster sugar and the almonds, if using. Bake the pudding in the centre of the oven for 40–45 minutes until the sponge is well-risen and golden brown. Serve hot with cream or home-made custard, sprinkled with a little extra sugar if you like.

VANILLA CUSTARD
Put the egg yolks in a medium saucepan with the cornflour and sugar. Scrape the vanilla seeds into the pan, or add the vanilla extract, and use a metal whisk to combine all the ingredients. Gradually whisk in the milk and cream.

Put the pan over a low heat and cook gently for 6–8 minutes, whisking constantly until the custard is smooth and thick. Do not allow it to overheat.

FRUITY MILK JELLY

A kids' favourite that was popular with lots of mums in the 1970s. You can either make it with normal whole milk or evaporated milk. Both work well, but the evaporated milk version tastes slightly creamier. Make sure you cool the jelly for a few minutes before stirring in the milk, as it will be less likely to separate.

SERVES 4–6

1 x 135g packet of orange or strawberry flavour jelly
1 x 410g can of fruit cocktail in syrup or juice
400ml whole milk or
1 x 410g can of evaporated milk

Break the jelly into cubes and put it in a measuring jug. Pour over enough just-boiled water to bring the liquid up to the 200ml mark. Stir well with a fork until all the jelly dissolves. Set aside to cool for about 5 minutes.

Drain the fruit cocktail, discard the liquid and put the fruit into a jelly mould. Stir the fresh or evaporated milk into the jelly until well combined – you'll feel it begin to thicken as you stir – then gently pour this on top of the fruit. Put the jelly in the fridge and chill until set. This will take about 4–6 hours.

ZIMWOMEN ASSOCIATION, NORTHAMPTONSHIRE

The Zimwomen Association was formed in 2009 to promote cultural identity and positive images of African women in the UK and to provide advice, social and cultural activities, education and training. The aim is to empower women, young people and children for a better today and tomorrow. Based in Northampton, the group was started by women from Zimbabwe but now includes members from many countries. Here are some favourite recipes from the group.

MANYATI'S VEGGIE CHILLI

SERVES 4

3 tbsp olive oil
1 small onion, chopped
2 carrots, diced
½ red, yellow and green pepper
100g green beans, chopped
2 tomatoes, chopped
3–4 chillies, deseeded and chopped
salt and pepper

Heat the oil in a large pan and gently fry the onion. Add the carrots, peppers and green beans and fry briefly. Now add the tomatoes, stir in the chopped chillies and simmer the stew until it is cooked to your liking. Season to taste and serve hot or cold. Any leftovers keep well in the fridge for up to 3 days.

PEANUT BUTTER VEGETABLES

SERVES 4

¼ small cabbage (or any vegetable in season), thinly cut
1 small onion, chopped
1 tomato, chopped
4 tbsp peanut butter
salt and pepper to taste

Pour about 120ml of water into a pan and bring to the boil. Add the cabbage and cook until softened but still crunchy. Then add the onion and tomato and season to taste. Stir in the peanut butter, adding more water if the mixture seems too thick. Season and serve with sadza (see below).

SADZA

SERVES 4

375g white cornmeal (mealie meal)

Mix 225g of cornmeal with 250ml of water. Bring 750ml of water to the boil in a pan, then turn down the heat and add the cornmeal mixture, stirring all the time. Cook for 5 minutes, then slowly add the rest of the cornmeal until the mixture is thick. Transfer to a bowl or plate and shape into a round with a wooden spoon.

Acknowledgments

First and foremost, we'd like to thank the mums, dads and families who appear in the programmes and provided recipes for this book: Anjie, Avis, Conolly, Dee, Derith, Elaine, Helen, Jayne, Jenny, Julia, Karen, Lisa, Marika, Mariken, Mary, Nancy, Padmaja, Polly, Rebecca, Rosalyn, Rosita, Ruth Joseph, Ruth Sutcliffe and Victoria.

At the recipe fairs we'd also like to thank the various community groups who fed and supported us – the Bath Place Community Venture, Studley Grow, Cook and Eat, the African Women's Group, Growing Together (St George's Community Hub), Lift Community Trust, Nepalese Community Oxfordshire, Slow Food and the Zimwomen Association. Thanks must also go to more than a thousand mums and families who turned up with their treasures at our fairs. Without them none of this would have been possible. And many thanks to our mate Gerard Baker, to Toti Gifford and his magical circus folks, and to Claire Bassano, Nikki Morgan and Kylie Morris.

Back at the Mailbox mothership, huge thanks to Nick Patten, head of studio BBC Birmingham, Gill Tierney, our executive producer, and editors James Cole, Andrew McKenzie, Louise Pearson, Martin Sage, Ant Smith, Kate Davis and Benedict Peissel.

Special thanks to our old friend and colleague from Hairy Baker days Oliver Clark, series producer, and our directors Duncan Barnes, Becky Pratt, Dan Slee, Joanna Brame and Francois Gandolfi.

On the road, we'd like to thank our production manager Sarah Greene, researchers Joe Barrett, Jean Campbell and Keaton Stone, and production coordinators Ella Gutteridge and Alison Davy. Also thanks to our great cameramen Roger Laxon, Craig Jones, Jon Boast, Stu Dunn, Adrian Croome and Tom Slee for making us look presentable, and to our sound men James Baker, Mark Skilton, Paul Scurrell and Andy Morton. Thanks also to Tim Jones, Max Beats, Avone Keene, Andy Darbyshire and Anton Inwood and everyone else involved in making the programme happen.

Last but not least, we owe a huge debt of gratitude to our home economist and good friend Sammy-Jo Squire.

Thanks, too, to MOTO-GUZZI, Phil Read and Mark Hemmingway for help with our lovely bikes.

We are very proud of this book and much credit for this must go once again to our friends at Orion. Thanks to the lovely Amanda Harris, Lucie Stericker for her skill and for letting us wreck her kitchen, Kate Barr for her gorgeous design, and Jinny Johnson for her patience and command of the English language. A huge thank you to Cristian Barnett and his assistant Roy Baron for the fab photographs and to Sammy-Jo and her assistant Nikki Morgan for all their hard work making the food for the book.

And, of course, as well as all these lovely folk, we'd like to thank our wonderful families for putting up with the pair of us.

Si & Dave

Nancy

Ruth Sutcliffe

Lisa

Je

Polly

Mary

Ma

Ruth Joseph

Helen

Rebecca

Anjie

Padmaja

Karen